Lab Manual for MCSE Guide to

Managing a Microsoft® Windows® Server 2003 Network

Ron Carswell

THOMSON
™
COURSE TECHNOLOGY

Australia • Canada • Mexico • Singapore • Spain • United Kingdom • United States

Lab Manual for MCSE Guide to Managing a Microsoft Windows Server 2003 Network

by Ron Carswell

Managing Editor:
Will Pitkin III

Product Manager:
Nick Lombardi

Production Editor:
Brooke Booth

Technical Edit/Quality Assurance:
Marianne Snow
Serge Palladino
Danielle Shaw

Associate Product Manager:
Mirella Misiaszek
David Rivera

Editorial Assistant:
Amanda Piantedosi

Senior Manufacturing Coordinator:
Trevor Kallop

Senior Marketing Manager:
Jason Sakos

Text Designer:
GEX Publishing Services

Compositor:
GEX Publishing Services

Cover Design:
Steve Deschene

TABLE OF
Contents

CHAPTER 3

TCP/IP Architecture **41**

CHAPTER 7

Implementing and Managing the DNS Service 117

CHAPTER 8

Implementing and Managing WINS   **137**

CHAPTER 11

Internet Authentication Service **193**

CHAPTER 12

CHAPTER 13

CHAPTER 14

Introduction

The objective of this lab manual is to assist you in preparing for the Microsoft Certification Exam 70-291: Implementing, Managing, and Maintaining a Microsoft Windows Server 2003 Network Infrastructure by applying the Windows Server 2003 objectives to relevant lab activities. This text is designed to be used in conjunction with *MCSE Guide to Managing a Microsoft Windows Server 2003 Network* (0-619-12029-0), and it should be noted that many of the labs rely upon activities from the *MCSE Guide* being completed first. Without completing those activities first, students may get different results from the labs. Although this manual is written to be used in a classroom lab environment, it also may be used for self-study on a home network.

This manual provides you with the information you need to install and manage network services on a Windows Server 2003 network. Each chapter presents a series of labs with different networking protocols or services that support learning of relevant skills for the management of a modern day network. Your instructor will provide you with answers to the review questions and additional information about the activities. Although designed to be used in a classroom environment, the lab activities can be easily modified to work within the confines of your own home network. Please review the setup information on what may be necessary to perform the labs in a test environment at home.

Features

In order to ensure a successful experience for instructors and students alike, this book includes the following features:

- **Lab Objectives** – The goal of each lab is clearly stated at the beginning.
- **Materials Required** – Every lab includes information on hardware, software, and other materials that you will need to complete the lab.
- **Estimated Completion Time** – Every lab has an estimated completion time, so that you can plan your activities more accurately.
- **Activity Background** – Activity Background information provides important details and prepares students for the activity that follows.
- **Activity Sections** – Labs are presented in manageable sections and include figures to reinforce learning.
- **Step-by-Step Instructions** – Steps provide practice, which enhances technical proficiency.

- **Microsoft Windows Server 2003 MCSE Certification Objectives** – For each chapter, the relevant objectives from MCSE Exam # 70-291 are listed.
- **Review Questions** – Review reinforces concepts presented in the lab.

Hardware requirements

All hardware in the computer should be listed on the Hardware Compatibility List available at *www.microsoft.com*.

Operating System	Microsoft Windows Server 2003
CPU	Pentium 400MHz or higher (Pentium III 550MHz is recommended)
Memory	128 MB RAM (256 MB RAM recommended)
Disk Space	Minimum of two 4-GB partitions (C and D), with at least 4 GB of free space left on the drive for student exercises
Drives	CD-ROM Floppy Disk
Networking	All lab computers should be networked. Students will work in pairs for some lab exercises. A connection to the Internet via some sort of NAT or Proxy server is assumed.
Monitor	SVGA or better resolution monitor

Software Requirements

The following software is needed for proper setup of the labs:

- Microsoft Windows Server 2003, Enterprise Edition or Standard Edition

Setup Procedure

Initially, each pair of students will require two computers. For Chapters 1 through 8, install Microsoft Windows Server 2003 as illustrated in the figure below.

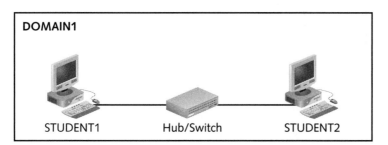

Throughout the lab activities, the first server uses Student1 as the computer name, and the second server uses Student2. Although the naming schemes remain consistent throughout the initial lab activities, you should feel free to change names based on your classroom environment. In a classroom environment, you will be required to issue students computer names that are unique. It is suggested that you start with the base names above and then modify the sequence numbers.

Chapter 9, Securing Network Traffic, will require the Student1, Student2, and the Student4 servers to be on the same 192.168.1.0 segment. The Student4 server will be borrowed from the second team for this lab.

Chapter 10, Remote Access, and Chapter 11, Internet Authentication Server, require a modem and a modem line for each server. If necessary, you could use a null modem cable. Also, a telco line simulator could be used to facilitate the modem line and PBX.

Chapter 12, Routing, presents some special challenges, as three LAN segments are required for the labs on IP routing. By combining the servers for two teams, the required four servers are available. The following figure provides the network diagram for these four servers.

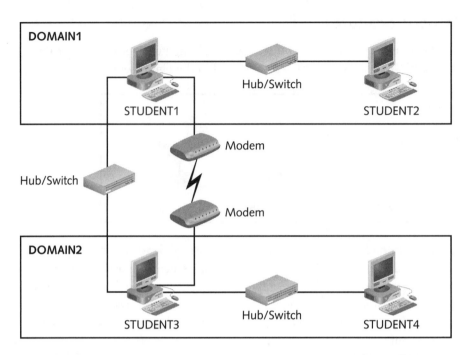

This table identifies each team's computer names and the respective IP addresses to be used for Chapter 12, Routing.

Server	Pod	Team	Domain	Primary IP Address	Secondary IP Address
Student1	1	1	Domain1	192.168.1.1	192.168.3.1
Student2	1	1	Domain1	192.168.1.2	-
Student3	1	2	Domain2	192.168.2.1	192.168.3.2
Student4	1	2	Domain2	192.168.2.2	-
Student5	2	3	Domain3	192.168.3.1	192.168.5.1
Student6	2	3	Domain3	192.168.3.2	-
Student7	2	4	Domain4	192.168.4.1	192.168.5.2
Student8	2	4	Domain4	192.168.4.2	-
Student9	3	5	Domain5	192.168.5.1	192.168.7.1
Student10	3	5	Domain5	192.168.5.2	-
Student11	3	6	Domain6	192.168.6.1	192.168.7.2
Student12	3	6	Domain6	192.168.6.2	-
Student13	4	7	Domain7	192.168.7.1	192.168.9.1
Student14	4	7	Domain7	192.168.7.2	-
Student15	4	8	Domain8	192.168.8.1	192.168.9.2
Student16	4	8	Domain8	192.168.8.2	-

Chapter 13, Security Templates, and Chapter 14, Troubleshooting Network Connectivity, require the setup used for the first eight labs.

ACKNOWLEDGEMENTS

I would like to thank the following reviewers, whose insightful comments have proven invaluable in the development of this manual:

Patty Gillilan	Sinclair Community College
CJ Gray	Pittsburg Technical Institute
Robert Sherman	Sinclair Community College
Duncan Ton	Minneapolis Community and Technical College

I would also like to thank my wife, Coleen, for the numerous hours devoted to testing each lab. Her insight, from a student perspective, enhanced the quality of the lab activities.

–Ron Carswell

1

NETWORKING OVERVIEW

Labs included in this chapter:

♦ 1.1 Overview of Networks and Network Infrastructures

♦ 1.2 Connecting to Networks

Microsoft MCSE Exam #70-291 Objectives	
Objective	Lab
Configure TCP/IP addressing on a server computer.	1.1, 1.2

Lab 1.1 Overview of Networks and Network Infrastructures

Objectives

The goal of this lab is to describe the various network scales and to differentiate between the three network architectures.

Materials Required

This lab will require the following:

- A pen or pencil and a sheet of paper

Estimated completion time: **15 minutes**

Activity Background

Simply stated, a network is a series of computer devices or nodes interconnected by communication paths. Of course, networks can grow to interconnect with other networks. Likewise, networks can contain smaller collections of nodes called subnetworks.

Network size can grow from a pair of computers in the den of your home to thousands of computers for a multinational corporation.

The Small Office Home Office (SOHO) network serves the needs of the small or home office environment. The home entrepreneur can purchase a minimum amount of equipment and enjoy the benefits of the SOHO network. In Figure 1-1, the components for the SOHO are pictured. At the top of the figure, there is the DSL/cable modem, which connects to the Internet. The router secures the local network and provides connectivity for the two computers. Of course, the printer provides print capability for the network.

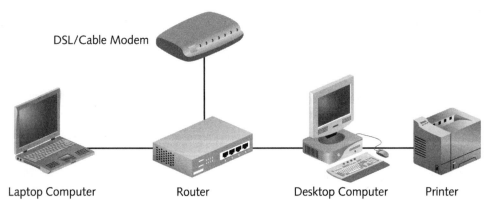

Figure 1-1   Small Office Home Office (SOHO) network

Here are the requirements for the SOHO network:

- An Internet connection provided by the local telephone or cable company

- A router with a switch that connects your local area network (LAN) to the Internet through your DSL (Digital Subscriber Line) modem or cable modem. The router provides a number of security features to protect both your network and the users of your network.

- A computer or computers with Ethernet capability. Newer computer models have Ethernet connections built in. If you do not see an Ethernet jack, you need to purchase an Ethernet NIC (network interface card).

- An Ethernet patch cable to connect each computer to the switch ports on the router.

- A printer (optional)

As your company grows, you will want your network to grow to meet the expanded needs of your company. Additional desktop computers will need to be added with more servers to support the increased number of users. If users travel away from the office, remote access will be required.

A medium-sized office network has the following characteristics:

- At least 250 desktop and laptop computers

- Servers to support application and storage requirements

- Several LAN segments with a backbone with one LAN segment on each floor or wing of a building

- Routers joining the various WAN/LAN segments

- Switches delivering traffic to the various desktop computers

- Dial-up connections supporting users who connect from home or while traveling out of town

- Internet connections through a firewall that protects the local network

Figure 1-2 shows an example of a medium-sized office network.

A medium-sized office network typically uses a few different types of network media. The different office segments can use 100 Mbps Ethernet. The backbone network that is used to connect to the different networks and host servers can use 1000 Mbps or GB Ethernet.

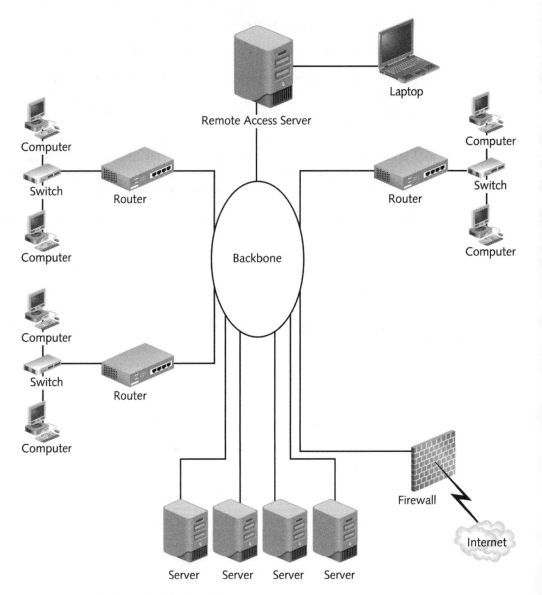

Figure 1-2 Medium-sized network

As your company grows geographically, you will want to expand the network to include the various remote offices.

Challenges exist to interconnect a company's multiple offices as they are geographically dispersed. Subnetworks require interconnection over vast distances. A remote office could approach the size of a medium network. A central office could grow in magnitude.

A large network has the following characteristics:

- At least 2,400 desktop and laptop computers

■ Additional servers to support the increased application and storage requirements

■ Multiple special application servers for databases and Web support

■ A requirement for server redundancy for mission critical applications

■ High-speed wide area network (WAN) connections

Figure 1-3 shows an example of a large network.

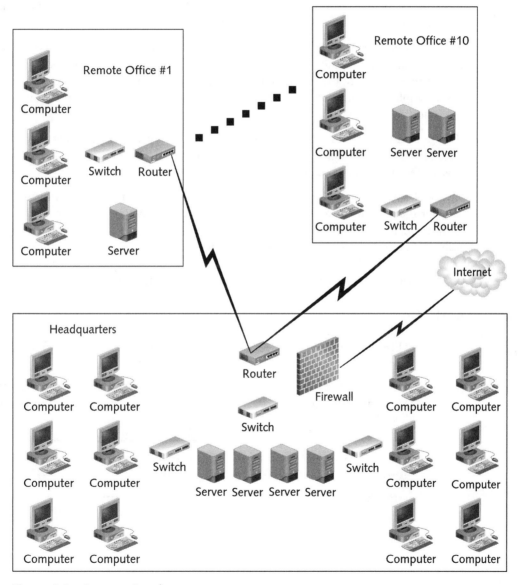

Figure 1-3 Large network

A LAN (local area network) is a group of computers, switches, and routers that share a common communications line or wireless link. The scope of the network is limited to a small geographic area (for example, within an office building). Usually, applications and data storage are provided by one or more servers that are shared by multiple computer users. A local area network may serve as few as two or three users (for example, in a SOHO network) or as many as hundreds of users (for example, in a medium network).

A suite of application programs can typically be stored on a LAN server. Users submit print jobs for printers and other services as needed through applications run from a LAN server. Files can be shared with multiple users of a LAN server. A LAN administrator maintains security access to the resources on a LAN server.

A metropolitan area network (MAN) is a network that interconnects users and computer resources in a geographic area larger than that covered by even a large local area network. The term is applied to the interconnection of networks in a city into a single larger network. For example, a medical organization with multiple interconnected clinics conforms to the definition of a WAN.

This term is also used to mean the interconnection of several local area networks by routing over communication lines. Since this networking model first appeared on university campus, it is sometimes referred to as a campus network.

A WAN (wide area network) is a geographically dispersed telecommunications network. The term distinguishes a broader telecommunication structure from a local area network. A WAN may be privately owned or rented, but the term usually connotes the inclusion of public (shared user) networks. Companies incorporate carrier lines rented from telephone companies and other communication providers. As an alternative to carrier lines, frame relay provides connectivity using shared communication resources.

ACTIVITY

Activity

1. List the names of five items that you would need to purchase to set up a small network in your home.

   _____

2. List the four differences between a SOHO network and a medium-sized network.

   _____

3. List five challenges that you would have to overcome as your company's network grows from a medium-sized to a large network.

   _____

4. Match the stated characteristics with the network architecture.

Network Architecture	Characteristics
1. LAN _____	a. Devices share a single Ethernet segment
2. MAN _____	b. Computers share an Internet connection
3. WAN _____	c. Offices connect to a central site in a large city
	d. Public shared communications lines are used to connect multiple cities
	e. Company's servers are located in each office

Certification Objectives

Objectives for Microsoft MCSE Exam #70-291: Implementing, Managing, and Maintaining a Microsoft Windows Server 2003 Network Infrastructure:

■ Configure TCP/IP addressing on a server computer.

REVIEW QUESTIONS

1. It is a normal day at school. You walk up to an ongoing discussion with your two close friends, Mike and Lillie. They are discussing how to set up a SOHO for their three personal computers. They ask you to summarize information about the equipment required to establish a SOHO. Which of the following will you include in your summary? (Choose all that apply.)

   a. Subscription to an Internet service provider (ISP) with cable or DSL services

   b. Eight-port Ethernet hub or switch

   c. Router with firewall and four-port switch

   d. Token Ring NICs for the three personal computers

   e. Three Ethernet patch cables

   f. Microsoft Windows Server 2003 Enterprise Edition

2. You are on the networking team for Fast–Growing, Inc. The company plans to expand from the single existing location, which houses the headquarters, to multiple locations with regional offices on both coasts. You are asked to formulate a growth strategy for the networking team. Which of the following items will you include in your proposal? (Choose all that apply.)

   a. Increased numbers of desktop computers

   b. Remote access for the sales personnel

   c. Web servers for the customer information center

   d. Redundant database servers for the ordering system

   e. High-speed communications between the regional offices and the headquarters

   f. Firewall for Internet connection

LAB 1.2 CONNECTING TO NETWORKS

Objectives

The goal of this lab is to describe the Open Systems Interconnection (OSI) reference model with respect to the identity of each layer. An additional goal includes describing network cabling types and network topologies. Also, describing network and transport protocols is a goal of this lab.

Materials Required

This lab will require the following:

- A pen or pencil and a sheet of paper

Estimated completion time: **15 minutes**

Activity Background

The OSI model is a standard reference model that displays the communication between two end users in a network. Instructors use it to help students to understand networks. The writers of standards use the model to specify how hardware and software systems should function. You must know the functionality of the OSI model to successfully answer exam questions related to networking.

The OSI model defines networking in terms of a vertical stack of seven layers. The four upper layers of the OSI model represent software that implements network services, such as applications and connection management. The lower layers of OSI implement more primitive functions, such as routing, addressing, and flow control.

In summary, the OSI model divides the big task of node-to-node networking into a vertical stack. The OSI model contains these seven layers (in order from top to bottom):

Upper layers

7. Application

6. Presentation

5. Session

Lower layers

4. Transport

3. Network

2. Data Link

1. Physical

The layered approach to OSI offers several advantages to system administrators. The OSI model allows the network administrator to arrange networking terminology structurally. By breaking the job of networking into logical smaller pieces, system administrators can more easily solve network "problems" through divide-and-conquer.

TIP   To remember the sequence of the OSI layers, recall the learning aid "All People Seem To Need Data Processing." Or if you may prefer going from bottom-to-top, recall "Please Do Not Throw Sausage Pizza Away."

The Physical layer defines the electrical, mechanical, procedural, and functional specifications for activating, maintaining, and deactivating the physical link between communicating network nodes. Voltage levels, timing of voltage changes, physical data rates, maximum transmission distances, physical connectors, and other similar attributes are defined by the Physical layer.

The Data Link layer permits reliable transit of data across a physical network link. Different Data Link layer specifications define different network and protocol characteristics. For example, physical addressing defines how devices are addressed at the Data Link layer using media access control (MAC) addressing. Network topology consists of the Data Link layer specifications that often define how devices are to be physically connected.

The Network layer defines the logical network address, which differs from the physical MAC address. Some Network layer implementations, such as the Internet Protocol (IP), define network addresses in a way that route selection can be determined systematically by comparing the source network address with the destination network address.

The Transport layer accepts data from the Network layer and reassembles the data after transport across the network. Generally, the Transport layer is responsible for those activities that make sure that the data is delivered error-free and in the proper sequence.

The Session layer establishes, manages, and terminates communication sessions. Communication sessions consist of service requests and service responses that occur between applications located in different network nodes. These requests and responses are coordinated by protocols implemented at the Session layer.

The Presentation layer provides a variety of coding and conversion functions that are applied to Session layer data. These functions ensure that information sent from the Application layer of one system would be readable by the Application layer of another system.

NOTE   If both computer operating systems are the same, the Presentation layer would not perform any coding or conversion functions.

The Application layer is the OSI layer closest to the end user, which means that both the Application layer and the user interact directly with the software application.

NOTE   This layer interacts with software applications that implement a communicating component. Application programs, such as word processing, fall outside the scope of the OSI reference model.

Network Topologies

A bus network is an arrangement in a LAN in which each node is connected to a main cable called the bus. Figure 1-4 shows a bus network with five nodes.

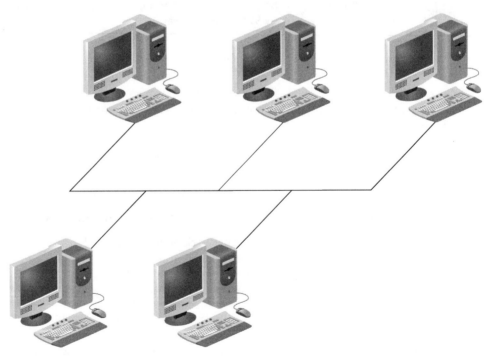

Figure 1-4   Bus network

A bus network is simple and reliable. If one node fails to operate, all the rest can still communicate with each other. For a major disruption to take place, the bus itself must be broken or a connector broken. Bus networks are easy to expand. Additional nodes can be added anywhere along the bus.

1

There are several limitations to the bus network topology. The length of the bus is limited by cable signal loss. A bus network may not work well if the nodes are located at scattered points that do not lie near a common line.

A star network is a LAN in which all nodes connect to a common node. Figure 1-5 shows a star network with five nodes. The LAN connections can be wired or wireless links.

The star network topology works well when workstations are at scattered points. It is easy to add or remove workstations.

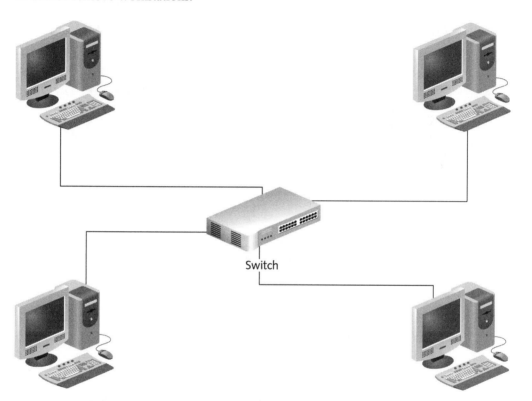

Figure 1-5   Star network

In a star network, a cable failure will isolate the node that it links to the common node, but only that node will be isolated. All the other nodes will continue to function normally, except that they will not be able to communicate with the isolated node. If any node goes down, none of the other nodes will be affected. But if the central node goes down, the entire network will suffer a complete failure.

A ring network is a LAN in which the nodes are connected in a closed loop configuration. Adjacent pairs of nodes are directly connected and repeat data between nodes. Other pairs of nodes are indirectly connected with the data passing through one or more intermediate nodes. Figure 1-6 shows a ring network with five nodes.

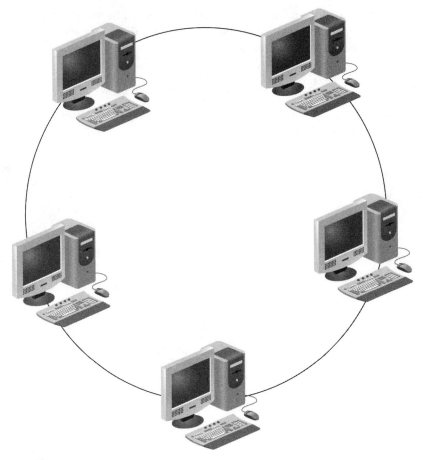

Figure 1-6   Ring network

A break in the cable results in a rerouting of frames to avoid the broken segment of the ring. This may result in degraded data speed between pairs of workstations for which the data path is increased as a result of the break. If two breaks occur, the entire network may suffer a complete failure.

Network Protocols

There are two network protocols that the network administrator may encounter. The Internet Protocol (IP) is a TCP/IP (Transmission Control Protocol/Internet Protocol) protocol at layer three of the OSI model. Likewise, the Novell Internetwork Packet eXchange (IPX) protocol resides at the Network layer.

IP is the Network layer protocol by which data is sent from one node to another on the Internet. Each node (known as a host) on the Internet has at least one IP address that uniquely identifies it from all other nodes on the Internet.

IP is a connectionless protocol, which means that there is no continuous connection between the nodes that are communicating. Each packet that travels through the Internet is treated as an independent unit of data without any relation to any other unit of data. IP is called an unreliable protocol. It is said that IP makes a "best effort" attempt to route the packet to the destination node but does not guarantee delivery.

IPX is a Network layer protocol from Novell that interconnects networks that use Novell's NetWare clients and servers. IPX works at the Network layer of the OSI model and like IP is connectionless. IPX controls addressing and routing of packets of data within and between networks.

NWLink is Microsoft's native 32-bit implementation of Novell's IPX/SPX protocol. NWLink supports two networking APIs (application programming interfaces): NetBIOS and WinSock. This protocol allows communications among computers running Windows Server 2003 and between computers running Windows Server 2003 and NetWare servers.

As you move up the OSI model, the next layer up from the Network layer is the Transport layer. Two Transport layer protocols that network administrators may encounter are TCP (Transmission Control Protocol) and Sequenced Packet eXchange (SPX).

Transport Protocols

TCP is a protocol used along with IP to send data in the form of data segments between nodes over the Internet. While IP takes care of handling the actual delivery of the data, TCP takes care of keeping track of the individual packets that a message is divided into for efficient routing through the Internet.

TCP is known as a connection-oriented protocol, which means that a connection is established and maintained until such time as the message or messages to be exchanged by the application programs at each end have been exchanged. TCP is responsible for ensuring that a message is divided into the packets that IP manages and for reassembling the packets back into the complete message at the other end. TCP is a reliable protocol and requires the receiving node to acknowledge the receipt of each packet.

The User Datagram Protocol (UDP) offers a limited amount of service when messages are exchanged between nodes. UDP is an alternative to TCP. Like TCP, UDP uses the IP to actually get a data unit (called a datagram) from one node to another. Unlike TCP, however, UDP does not provide the service of dividing a message into packets and reassembling it at the other end. This means that the application program that uses UDP must be able to make sure that the entire message has arrived and is in the right order. To save processing overhead, because your application has very small data units to exchange, you may prefer UDP's speed to TCP.

UDP is referred to as a connectionless, unreliable protocol. UDP does not set up a connection, as does TCP. In addition, UDP makes a "best effort" attempt at forwarding datagrams similar to the transfer of packets by IP.

SPX is the protocol for handling packet sequencing in a Novell NetWare network. SPX prepares the sequence of packets in which a message is divided and then manages the reassembly of received packets. In addition to handling packet sequencing, SPX confirms that all packages have been received and requests retransmission when they haven't. SPX works directly with IPX.

Activity

ACTIVITY

1. Name in correct sequence from bottom to top the seven layers of the OSI reference model.

   _____

2. Match the OSI reference model layer to the correct definition.

   OSI Layer
   1. Application _____
   2. Presentation _____
   3. Session _____
   4. Transport _____
   5. Network _____
   6. Data Link _____
   7. Physical _____

   Definition
   a. Electrical and functional specifications
   b. Physical addressing and network topology
   c. Logical addressing and supports routing
   d. Responsibility for delivery of data
   e. Establishes, manages, and terminates communications
   f. Conversion of data
   g. Interacts with the user's software

3. Match the network topology with the characteristics of the topology.

   Network Topology
   1. Bus _____
   2. Star _____
   3. Ring _____

   Characteristics
   a. Each node is connected to a main cable
   b. When a cable breaks, one node may cease to operate
   c. Nodes are connected in a closed loop.
   d. Each node is connected to a common point
   e. When a cable breaks, one nodes may reroute data
   f. Nodes repeat data
   g. When the cable breaks, all nodes may cease to operate

Certification Objectives

Objectives for Microsoft MCSE Exam #70-291: Implementing, Managing, and Maintaining a Microsoft Windows Server 2003 Network Infrastructure

■ Configure TCP/IP addressing on a server computer.

REVIEW QUESTIONS

1. You create a question for your networking study group. You hand the question to Mary. How will Mary respond to the question: What layer of the OSI model is responsible for packaging and transmitting data on an Ethernet cable?

   a. Session Layer

   b. Transmission Layer

   c. Transport Layer

   d. Data link Layer

   e. Physical Layer

2. You hand Mary your next question: At what layer would the functions of IP be defined? How will Mary respond to the question?

   a. Session Layer

   b. TCP/IP Layer

   c. Transport Layer

   d. Data link Layer

   e. Network Layer

3. You hand Mary your third question: At which layer of the OSI model would you be concerned with user applications, such as Microsoft Word or Excel?

   a. Application Layer

   b. Program Layer

   c. Suite Layer

   d. Transport Layer

   e. None

4. You are concerned by the alphabet soup of letters at the network layers and transport layers of the OSI model. You ask Juan for help. Which items will Juan indicate are valid?

   a. TCP and UDP are network protocols.

   b. TCP is a transport protocol.

   c. IPX resides at the same level as IP.

   d. IPX resides at the same level as TCP.

   e. SPX is a transport protocol.

   f. NWLink is TCP/IPX.

   g. NWLink is IPX/SPX.

5. You are a network administrator for a medium-sized corporation. You have been asked to review the network plan proposed by the new hire in the networking group. Refer to Figure 1-7 for the graphic details of the proposal. Indicate any correction or omission that the new hire might have made. (Choose all that apply.)

   a. Replace the Token Ring with a fiber distributed data interface (FDDI).

   b. Replace the router with a remote access server.

   c. Place a bridge on the Internet connection.

   d. Place a firewall on the Internet connection.

   e. Replace the Token Ring with an Ethernet.

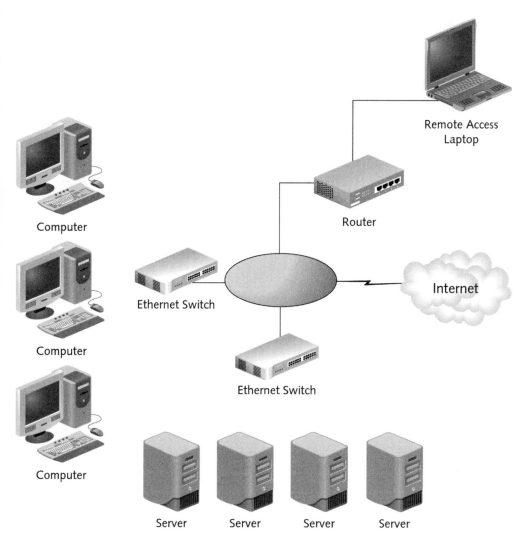

Figure 1-7   Networking proposal

2

IP ADDRESSING BASICS

Microsoft MCSE Exam #70-291 Objectives	
Objective	Lab
Configure TCP/IP addressing on a server computer.	2.1, 2.2, 2.3, 2.4, 2.5
Troubleshoot TCP/IP addressing.	2.5
Manage DHCP.	2.2, 2.3, 2.5

LAB 2.1 USING IP ADDRESSES

Objectives

The goal of this lab is to describe the IP address Classes A, B, and C for IP addressing. IP addresses are required for computers to communicate using IP on a network. As a networking administrator, you must be knowledgeable about IP addressing.

Materials Required

This lab will require the following:

- A pen or pencil

Estimated completion time: **20 minutes**

Activity Background

Each host or network node on an IP network requires a unique IP address or logical address. The logical IP address is a Network layer address.

Just as a street address includes a block and house number, an IP address includes a network ID and a host ID.

- All nodes on the same physical network segment must have the same network ID. You may consider routers as defining the gateways for off-segment communication. The network ID should not duplicate another network ID.

- Each node is assigned a host ID. The host address cannot duplicate another host address within the network ID.

An IP address consists of 32 binary digits. However, because it is difficult to work with binary numbers, the address is segmented into four 8-bit segments called octets, which are represented by a decimal number in the range 0 to 255. The Internet uses three address classes to accommodate networks of varying sizes. You probably will support networks with class A, B, and C addresses assigned to hosts. The class of address defines which bits of an IP address are used for the network ID and which bits are used for the host ID. It also defines the possible number of networks and the number of hosts per network.

Class A addresses are assigned to networks with a very large number of hosts. The first octet (8 bits) represents the network ID. The last three octets (24 bits) represent the host ID. This permits 126 networks and 16,777,214 hosts per network.

Class B addresses are assigned to medium-sized to large networks. The first two octets (16 bits) represent the network ID. The last two octets (16 bits) represent the host ID. This permits 16,384 networks and 65,534 hosts per network.

Class C addresses are used for small networks. The first three octets (24 bits) represent the network ID. The last octet (8 bits) represents the host ID. This allows for 2,097,152 networks and 254 hosts per network.

The network ID identifies the IP hosts that are located on the same physical network. For the hosts on a physical network to communicate with each other, you must assign the same network ID.

You should follow these guidelines when assigning a network ID:

- The network ID cannot be duplicated within your organization.

- If you do not plan to connect to the Internet, the local network ID must be unique only within your private intranet.

- If you plan to use public IP addresses on the Internet, the network ID must be unique within the Internet.

- The network ID of 127 is reserved to test the IP software stack (ping 127.0.0.1).

- All bits within the network ID cannot be set to 1 (IP broadcast address).

- All bits within the network ID cannot be set to 0 (specific host).

Table 2-1 lists the valid ranges of network IDs based on the IP address classes. To indicate IP network IDs, the host octets are all set to 0.

Table 2-1 Valid ranges for network IDs

Address Class	First Network ID	Last Network ID
Class A	1.0.0.0	126.0.0.0
Class B	128.0.0.0	191.255.0.0
Class C	192.0.0.0	223.255.255.0

A default subnet mask is used to tell an IP node which octets to use for the network ID. Each IP address class has a unique default subnet mask. Each host on an IP network requires a subnet mask.

The subnet mask is a 32-bit value that is used to indicate which bits belong to the network ID. By applying the subnet mask to an IP address, the bits (or octets) for the network ID can be extracted. The bits of the subnet mask are defined as follows:

- All bits that correspond to the network ID are set to 1.

- All bits that correspond to the host ID are set to 0.

Subnet masks are represented in dotted decimal notation. Although the subnet mask is created using dotted decimal notation, the subnet mask is not an IP address. Table 2-2 lists the default subnet masks using binary and dotted decimal notation.

Table 2-2 Default subnet masks

Address Class	Bits for Subnet Mask	Subnet Mask
Class A	11111111.00000000.00000000.00000000	255.0.0.0
Class B	11111111.11111111.00000000.00000000	255.255.0.0
Class C	11111111.11111111.11111111.00000000	255.255.255.0

To obtain a network ID, IP extracts the network ID from an IP address using the subnet mask as a pattern. IP compares, bit by bit, the bits in the IP address to the bits in the subnet mask. The result is 1 when both bits being compared are 1; otherwise the result is 0. This activity is summarized in Table 2-3.

Table 2-3 AND comparison table

	Bit	Bit	Bit	Bit
IP address bit	1	0	1	0
Subnet bit	1	1	0	0
Result	1	0	0	0

TIP

The process can be expressed in simple terms: Ones drop the IP address bit to the result. Zeroes block the IP address bit from the result.

ACTIVITY

Activity

1. Describe the following characteristics of Class A, Class B, and Class C IP addresses: Address range, the number of network bits, the number of host bits, and default subnet mask.

   _____

   _____

2. Briefly describe the five network IP guidelines.

   _____

   _____

3. Determine the network ID for each of the following IP addresses:

   12.23.67.35   255.0.0.0   _____

   135.12.45.198   255.255.0.0   _____

   198.23.12.45   255.255.255.0   _____

Certification Objectives

Objectives for MCSE Exam #70-291: Implementing, Managing, and Maintaining a Microsoft Windows Server 2003 Network:

■ Configure TCP/IP addressing on a server computer.

2

REVIEW QUESTIONS

1. On a network that uses the TCP/IP protocol, each node that has a logical IP address is also known as a _____.

   a. Peer

   b. Host

   c. Server

   d. Client

   e. Station

2. Which of the following IP addresses is a Class B address? (Choose all that apply.)

   a. 126.32.67.85

   b. 128.32.67.85

   c. 172.31.67.85

   d. 192.31.67.85

   e. 191.31.65.85

3. Which of the following is the default subnet mask for a Class C address?

   a. 255.0.0.0

   b. 255.255.0.0

   c. 255.255.255.0

   d. 255.255.254.0

   e. 255.255.255.255

4. Which of the following is the network ID for an IP address of 172.17.67.85 using the default subnet mask?

  a. 172.0.0.0

  b. 172.17.0.0

  c. 172.17.67.0

  d. 0.17.67.85

  e. 0.0.67.85

5. What of the following are the characteristics of a Class C IP address?

  a. Address range = 192–216, Network bits = 8, Host bits = 24

  b. Address range = 128–191, Network bits = 16, Host bits = 16

  c. Address range = 192–223, Network bits = 8, Host bits = 24

  d. Address range = 192–223, Network bits = 24, Host bits = 8

  e. Address range = 191–223, Network bits = 24, Host bits = 8

LAB 2.2 CREATING CUSTOM SUBNET MASKS

Objectives

The goal of this lab is to create custom subnet masks for a required number of subnets, which enable custom subnets to be designed. In addition, consideration will be made for the creation of custom subnet masks when host allocation is the criteria. As a networking administrator, you must be able to specify custom subnet masks.

Materials Required

This lab will require the following:

- A delta table

- A pen or pencil

Estimated completion time:**45 minutes**

Activity Background

You can use custom subnet masks to allocate IP addresses more effectively by:

- Dividing a large network into smaller networks.

- Reducing broadcasts by bounding each network with a router.

- Assigning a new subnet ID.

Custom subnet masks permit the creation of custom subnets. These subnets are subdivisions of an IP network, each with its own unique subnet ID. If you have "extra" bits in the host portion of the IP address, you can use these bits to create additional subnets.

Before you can calculate and apply subnet masks that meet the needs of network requirements, you need to create a process table called a delta table. A delta table will help reduce the complexity of calculations for the creation of custom subnet masks. An example of a delta table is shown in Table 2-4.

Table 2-4   Delta table for subnet masks

Bits	1	2	3	4	5	6	7	8
Delta values	128	64	32	16	8	4	2	1
Subnet masks	128	192	224	240	248	252	254	255

This delta table consists of three rows and eight columns. The first row is numbered from 1 through 8 with one column for each bit position in an octet.

The second row consists of the delta values, or bit values. You can generate the delta values by following these steps:

1. Enter 128 under the 1–bit column.

2. Enter half of the preceding value in the 2–bit column (that is, 128 divided by 2, which is equal to 64).

3. Repeat Step 2 for the renaming values by entering half the value of each preceding value in the remaining columns.

The third row consists of the subnet mask values. You can generate the subnet mask values by following these steps:

1. Enter 128 in the 1–bit column.

2. In the 2–bit column, enter the sum of the preceding value and the delta value (that is, 128 and 64 is equal to 192).

3. Repeat the process for the remaining values, adding the preceding value and the delta value.

Once you have completed your delta table, you can use it to determine custom subnet masks. You use the first row to locate the number of bits for the conversion process. You use the second row to create the values in the third row. In addition, you use the second row to calculate the resultant subnets. Using the values in the third row, you can select the appropriate subnet mask.

You can expand the delta table to indicate the maximum number of subnets available for each bit option. To expand the table, you insert a row directly below the first row. To fill in the values for each column, enter the value of 2 raised to the power indicated by the number of bits. Next you must subtract 2 from each calculation, because all bits in the network ID cannot be set to 1 or 0. For example, the value in the first column is 0, because 2 raised to the power of 1 is 2 minus 2. Likewise, the value in the second column is 2, because 2 raised to the second power is 4 minus 2. Table 2-5 shows the expanded delta table.

Table 2-5   Updated delta table with maximum quantity added

Bits	1	2	3	4	5	6	7	8
Maximum quantity	0	2	6	14	30	62	126	254
Delta values	128	64	32	16	8	4	2	1
Subnet masks	128	192	224	240	248	252	254	255

To use the delta table, you need to follow these guidelines:

1. Read across the second row to find for the first number that meets or exceeds the number of subnets that you need.

2. Read down the column to the third row to locate the delta value.

3. Read down the column to the fourth row to locate the required subnet mask.

If you need more than 254 subnets, you can expand the delta table.

To create a subnet mask for a given number of subnets, you begin with a design requirement. You work through the three-step process to determine a subnet mask.

Suppose that you are a designing a private network. You select the 172.19.0.0 private B address, which has 16 bits for the network and 16 bits for the hosts. You review your design requirements and determine that 10 subnets will fit your needs. You have created your delta table (Table 2-5) so you are ready.

First you read across the delta table to find the number that satisfies the requirement for 10 subnets, which is 14. Next you read down the column for the delta value, which is 16. Then you read down the column for the subnet mask, which is 240.

By determining a subnet mask of 4 bits, or 240, you have added four bits to the network. There are 20 bits (16 + 4 = 20) in the network and 12 bits (4 + 8 = 12) for hosts.

Consider a larger organization that requires a large number of subnets. The network planners have determined that 1000 subnets are needed. They have also decided to use the private 10.0.0.0 network, which affords the largest number of host bits at 24 bits.

To determine the correct subnet mask for the planners, you must expand the delta table for values that are equal to or greater then 1000. Then read across the second row to find 1000. But this time you need to go to the next number, which is 1022. Then you read down the column to the delta value of 64, and then read down the column again to find a subnet mask of 255.192. The correct subnet mask is 255.255.192.0.

2

Activity

ACTIVITY

1. Define the subnet mask for this situation:

   Given: Network 172.16.0.0

   Requirement: 12 subnets

   Complete the following entries:

   Maximum number from delta table: _____

   Number of bits from delta table: _____

   Subnet mask from delta table: _____

   Default Subnet Mask for 172.16.0.0: _____

   Custom Subnet mask that meets requirements: **255.255.240.0**

2. Define the subnet mask for each example below:

Network	Default Mask	Number of Subnets	Maximum Number	Number of Bits	Subnet Mask
172.16.0.0	255.255.0.0	5	6	3	255.255.224.0
172.17.0.0		50			
172.18.0.0		500		9	
192.168.23.0	255.255.255.0	10			
192.168.24.0		25			
10.0.0.0		4000			255.255.240.0

Certification Objectives

Objectives for MCSE Exam #70-291: Implementing, Managing, and Maintaining a Microsoft Windows Server 2003 Network:

- Configure TCP/IP addressing on a server computer.

- Manage DHCP.

REVIEW QUESTIONS

1. Blue Sky has been assigned a Class C network address of 195.110.160.0. As the network administrator, you have assigned a subnet mask of 255.255.255.224. How many subnets are possible with this configuration?

   a. 8 subnets

   b. 6 subnets

   c. 3 subnets

2. You have 25 sites and expect to grow to 45 in three years. Which subnet mask will provide enough subnets with the maximum number of hosts?

   a. 255.255.252.0

   b. 255.255.254.0

   c. 255.255.240.0

   d. 255.255.128.0

   e. 255.255.64.0

3. You have a system with 30 networks that will grow to 50. Which subnet mask will provide enough network IDs?

   a. 255.255.255.0

   b. 255.255.252.0

   c. 255.255.254.0

   d. 254.0.0.0

4. Johns Industries has a network address of 171.110.0.0. It needs 36 subnets with a minimum of 600 nodes per subnet. Which of the subnet masks below will meet these requirements?

   a. 255.255.252.0

   b. 255.255.192.0

   c. 255.255.255.0

   d. 255.255.248.0

5. You are a network administrator and have been assigned the IP address of 196.222.5.0. You need to have 20 subnets with 5 hosts per subnet. What subnet mask will you use?

   a. 255.255.255.248

   b. 255.255.255.128

   c. 255.255.255.192

   d. 255.255.255.240

LAB 2.3 CREATING SUBNETS AND HOSTS RANGES

Objectives

The goal of this lab is to specify custom subnets to meet your design requirements. In addition, you will specify host ranges. As a networking administrator, you must be able to specify host ranges.

Materials Required

This lab will require the following:

- A delta table

- A pen or pencil

Estimated completion time: **30 minutes**

Activity Background

When creating custom subnets, you need to determine the number of bits that are required for the hosts on each subnet and subtract the number of bits required for hosts from the number of bits available. The result is the number of bits required for the custom subnet mask.

Suppose you are a designing a private network. You select the 192.168.1.0 private C address. You survey your requirements and determine that 25 hosts per subnet will fit the future needs of the network. You read across your delta table and find the value of 30, which is the number that satisfies the requirement for 25 hosts. Reading down the column, you can see that 30 hosts require 5 bits. If you use the 8 bits of the fourth octet, 8 bits minus 5 bits is equal to 3 bits for the subnet mask. Using the delta table, you read across to 3 bits and down to the subnet mask of 224. The subnet mask of 224 requires 3 bits or columns in the delta table: the 128 bit, the 64 bit and the 32 bit.

After determining the subnet mask, you specify the subnet numbers. To calculate the first subnet for the private network, you add 32 (the delta value) to the fourth octet of the assigned network number.

```
192.  168.  1.   0
  0.    0.  0.   32
192.  168.  1.   32
```

For the remaining networks, add the delta value.

Now you need to specify the host IP addresses for each subnet. Recall that a host cannot have a value of all 0's or all 1's. This means that two IP addresses must be excluded from the range of host IP addresses.

You have determined that a subnet mask of 224 meets your needs for the private IP address of 192.168.1.0. Checking your delta table, you can see that a delta value of 32 corresponds to a subnet mask of 224. To calculate the first available host, you must add 1 to the subnet.

To determine the last host in a range, you must subtract 2 from the next subnet. You must leave the address for the local subnet broadcast to which no host can be assigned. The broadcast address for each subnet is the highest address and must always be an odd number.

To calculate the remaining host ranges, you follow these steps to:

- Add 1 to the current subnet.

- Subtract 2 from the next subnet.

 For the last available host address on the last valid subnet, subtract 2 from the subnet mask.

TIP

Before you create host ranges across multiple octets, you must use base 256 arithmetic. You need to subtract 2 from the IP address. In the following example, you cannot subtract 2 from 0, so you need to borrow 265 from the octet to the left. Applying the borrowing principle used in simple subtraction, you reduce the number of the column to the left by 1, while increasing the number in the right-hand column by 256. Then you can subtract 2 from 256.

```
            63.  256
172.  20.  ~~64~~.  0
 -0.   0.   0.  2
172.  20.  63.  254
```

When you borrow bits from another octet, you always borrow 256, decreasing the octet in that column by 1.

You have determined that a subnet mask of 224 meets your needs for the private IP address of 172.22.0.0 with a subnet mask of 255.255.224.0. You've checked your delta table to find that a delta value of 32 corresponds to a subnet mask of 224. Then to determine the host ranges, you added 1 to the current subnet and then subtracted 2 from the next network.

Activity

1. Specify the subnet numbers for the following situation:

   Given: Network 172.16.0.0

   Requirement: 6 subnets

   Custom subnet mask that meets requirements: 255.255.224.0

   Delta value from delta table: _____

~~172.16.0.0~~
172.16.96.0
~~172.16.224.0~~

2. Calculate the first four valid network numbers for each situation below.

Network	Subnet Mask	Delta Value	Network #1	Network #2	Network #3	Network #4
172.16.0.0	255.255.240.0	16	172.16.16.0	172.16.32.0	172.16.48.0	172.16.64.0
172.17.0.0	255.255.248.0	8	172.17.8.0			
172.18.0.0	255.255.252.0				172.18.12.0	
192.168.24.0	255.255.255.224			192.168.24.64		
10.0.0.0	255.224.0.0					10.128.0.0

3. Specify the host ranges for the first subnet.

   Given: Network 172.16.0.0

   Requirement: 6 subnets

   Custom subnet mask that meets requirements: 255.255.224.0

   Delta value from delta table: 32

   First two valid networks: 172.16.32.0 172.16.64.0

   First Host: _____

   Last Host: _____

4. Calculate the host range for the first network for each example below.

Network	Subnet Mask	Delta Value	First Network	Host Range	
172.16.0.0	255.255.255.0	1	172.16.1.0	172.16.1.1	172.16.1.254
172.17.0.0	255.255.224.0		172.17.32.0		
172.18.0.0	255.255.240.0				172.18.31.254
192.168.23.0	255.255.255.192				
10.0.0.0	255.240.0.0			10.16.0.1	
10.10.0.0	255.255.224.0	32			

Certification Objectives

Objectives for MCSE Exam #70-291: Implementing, Managing, and Maintaining a Microsoft Windows Server 2003 Network:

- Configure TCP/IP addressing on a server computer.

- Manage DHCP.

REVIEW QUESTIONS

1. You are the network administrator for the Jumbo Bakery, which bakes extra large pies. You have been assigned the network ID 192.168.85.0. You've determined that a subnet mask of 255.255.255.224 meets your requirements. Which of the following would be valid subnets for your network? (Choose all that apply.)

   a. 192.168.85.32

   b. 192.168.85.64

   c. 192.168.85.96

   d. 192.168.85.128

   e. 192.168.85.160

   f. 192.168.85.192

   g. 192.168.85.224

2. It has only been three months on the job, and you have been asked to develop the project plans for the new regional offices. You have worked through the calculations and have determined that you will use the Class B IP address 172.16.0.0, which was assigned to your company with a subnet mask of 255.255.252.0 You will need the first four subnets for your proposal. Which of the following will you include in your proposal? (Choose all that apply.)

 a. 172.16.2.0

 b. 172.16.4.0

 c. 172.16.6.0

 d. 172.16.8.0

 e. 172.16.10.0

 f. 172.16.12.0

 g. 172.16.14.0

 h. 172.16.16.0

3. You have been assigned network ID 192.168.22.0. You have determined that a subnet mask of 255.255.255.192 meets your requirements. You are ready to assign host IP addresses to your two subnets. Which of the following host ranges would be legal for your network? (Choose all that apply.)

 a. 192.168.22.65 − 192.168.22.94

 b. 192.168.22.65 − 192.168.22.126

 c. 192.168.22.97 − 192.168.22.126

 d. 192.168.22.129 − 192.168.22.158

 e. 192.168.22.129 − 192.168.22.190

4. Your proposal has been accepted. You had previously determined that you would use the Class B IP address 172.16.0.0 that was assigned to your company with a subnet mask of 255.255.252.0 You need the first host ranges for the first four subnets. Which of the following are legal for your network? (Choose all that apply.)

 a. 172.16.4.1 − 172.16.5.254

 b. 172.16.4.1 − 172.16.7.254

 c. 172.16.8.1 − 172.16.11.255

 d. 172.16.8.1 − 172.16.11.254

 e. 172.16.12.1 − 172.16.15.254

 f. 172.16.16.0 − 172.16.19.254

 g. 172.16.16.1 − 172.16.19.254

5. You have been assigned network ID 172.30.0.0. You have determined that a subnet mask of 255.255.224.0 meets your requirements. You are ready to assign host IP addresses to your six subnets. Which of the following host ranges would be legal for your network? (Choose all that apply.)

   a. 172.30.32.0 – 172.30.63.255

   b. 172.30.64.1 – 172.30.96.254

   c. 172.30.96.1 – 172.30.127.254

   d. 172.30.128.1 – 172.30.159.254

   e. 172.30.159.1 – 172.30.191.254

   f. 172.30.192.1 – 172.30.223.254

LAB 2.4 CREATING SUPERNETS

Objectives

The goal of this lab is to calculate supernets that combine multiple IP addresses to provide larger address spaces for hosts. As a networking administrator, you need to be knowledgeable regarding the creation of supernets.

Materials Required

This lab will require the following:

- A delta table

- A pen or pencil

Estimated completion time: **20 minutes**

Activity Background

Supernetting, also called classless interdomain routing (CIDR), is a way to aggregate multiple Internet addresses of the same class. Using supernetting, you merge network address 203.240.8.0 /24 and an adjacent address 203.240.9.0 /24 into 203.240.8.0 /23. The "23" at the end of the address says that the first 23 bits are the network part of the address, leaving the remaining nine bits for specific host addresses.

And how do you know what the CIDR of "/23" represents? To find out, first, you convert the 23 bits to a subnet mask of 255.255.254.0, as shown here:

```
8   + 8   + 7   = 23 Bits
255. 255. 254.0
```

Next, you locate the corresponding delta value of 2, which is the number of networks that are combined.

Consider another situation in which there are four networks and the ISP is given the following addresses:

```
194.12.4.0
194.12.5.0
194.12.6.0
194.12.7.0
```

To determine the correct CIDR, you need to read the delta table to find the subnet mask that corresponds to the delta value of 4, which is the subnet mask of 252. Next, you must determine the correct CIDR of 22 bits.

```
8   + 8   + 6   = 22 Bits
255. 255. 252.0
```

The combined network address is 192.12.4.0/22.

Activity

1. Develop a supernet that uses the following addresses:
```
192.168.8.0
192.168.9.0
192.168.10.0
192.168.11.0
```

_____

_____

2. Develop a supernet that uses the following addresses:
```
192.168.8.0
192.168.9.0
192.168.10.0
192.168.11.0
192.168.12.0
192.168.13.0
192.168.14.0
192.168.15.0
```

_____

Certification Objectives

Objectives for MCSE Exam #70-291: Implementing, Managing, and Maintaining a Microsoft Windows Server 2003 Network:

■ Configure TCP/IP addressing on a server computer.

REVIEW QUESTIONS

1. Which of the following is the correct subnet mask for the IP address 172.28.12.0/22?

   a. 255.255.248.0

   b. 255.255.255.252

   c. 255.255.252.0

   d. 255.255.248.0

   e. 255.252.0.0

2. How many valid host IP addresses are available on the subnet 172.16.100.24/30?

   a. 2

   b. 6

   c. 14

   d. 30

   e. 62

3. How many subnets are available on the subnet 172.16.64.0/20?

   a. 2

   b. 6

   c. 14

   d. 30

   e. 62

4. You are working for an ISP. It will be getting 1022 IP addresses starting at 204.112.8.0. What CIDR value do you use to supernet the addresses?

   a. /21

   b. /22

   c. /23

   d. /24

   e. /25

5. Your new ISP has received IP address 204.124.80.0/21. What are the first four supernets for this network? (Choose all that apply.)

    a. 204.124.76.0

    b. 204.124.80.0

    c. 204.124.81.0

    d. 204.124.0.0

    e. 204.124.82.0

    f. 204.124.82.254

    g. 204.124.83.0

LAB 2.5 TROUBLESHOOTING HOST RANGES

Objectives

The goal of this lab is to troubleshoot problems related to subnets and host ranges. Special attention is devoted to troubleshooting communication between computers. As a networking administrator, you must be capable of resolving IP addressing problems that prohibit computers from exchanging IP packets where IP configurations are incorrect.

Materials Required

This lab will require the following:

- A delta table

- A pen or pencil

Estimated completion time: **20 minutes**

Activity Background

One of the classic problems for a network administrator is to determine if two computers on the same physical segment can communicate with each other. Consider that you have two computers with the IP addresses of 192.168.5.135 and 192.168.5.156. The subnet mask is 255.255.255.224. Are the two computers on the same subnet?

To quickly calculate the subnet number on which 192.168.5.135 resides, you divide the host address by the delta number, and then multiply the quotient by the delta number, as shown here:

```
135 / 32 = 4 * 32 = 128
```

The results give you a subnet of 192.168.5.128.

Now you need to repeat the process for the second computer.

```
156 / 32 = 4 * 32 = 128
```

The subnet number is 128. Therefore, the two computers are on the same subnet and should communicate with each other.

Activity

1. Verify that the hosts are on a common subnet.

   Given: Host 172.16.45.10

          Host 172.16.49.10

          Subnet Mask: 255.255.248.0

   Delta value: _____

   Subnet number for first host: _____

   First host on subnet: _____

   Last host on subnet: _____

2. For the given network and subnet mask, determine whether the hosts are on the same subnet.

Network	Subnet Mask	Host A	Host B	Same Network
172.16.0.0	255.255.0.0	172.16.64.3	172.16.90.16	Y
172.17.0.0	255.255.248.0	172.16.12.3	172.16.20.7	
172.18.0.0	255.255.240.0	172.18.176.3	172.18.191.5	
172.19.0.0	255.255.254.0	172.19.22.3	172.19.25.3	
172.20.0.0	255.255.254.0	172.20.22.250	172.20.23.250	

Certification Objectives

Objectives for MCSE Exam #70-291: Implementing, Managing, and Maintaining a Microsoft Windows Server 2003 Network:

- Configure TCP/IP addressing on a server computer.

- Troubleshoot TCP/IP addressing.

- Manage DHCP.

REVIEW QUESTIONS

2

1. You are a network administrator and have been assigned the IP address of 201.2.5.0. You need to have 20 subnets with 5 hosts per subnet. The subnet mask is 255.255.255.248. Which of the following addresses are valid host addresses? (Choose all that apply.)

   a. 201.2.5.16

   b. 201.2.5.17

   c. 201.2.5.18

   d. 201.2.5.19

   e. 201.2.5.20

   f. 201.2.5.31

2. You have an IP host address of 201.2.5.121 and a subnet mask of 255.255.255.248. What is the broadcast address?

   a. 201.2.5.121

   b. 201.2.5.122

   c. 201.2.5.127

   d. 201.2.5.135

3. You have an IP host address of 172.18.65.83 with a subnet mask of 255.255.248.0. What is the subnet address?

   a. 172.18.0.0

   b. 172.18.65.0

   c. 172.18.64.0

   d. 172.18.96.0

   e. 172.18.248.0

4. Your computer's address is 172.16.35.100, and the subnet mask is 255.255.240.0. You are unable to communicate with another computer on the same subnet that has an IP address of 172.16.52.1 and a subnet mask of 255.255.240.0. What do you do to correct the problem?

a. Change the IP address of the second computer to 172.16.35.100.

b. Change the IP address of the second computer to 172.16.52.100.

c. Change the IP address of the second computer to an IP address in the range of 172.16.32.1 through 172.16.39.254.

d. Change the IP address of the second computer to an IP address in the range of 172.16.32.1 through 172.16.47.254.

5. You are given the following address: 128.16.32.13/30. Determine the subnet mask, address class, subnet address, and broadcast address.

a. 255.255.255.252, B,128.16.32.12, 128.16.32.15

b. 255.255.255.252, C,128.16.32.12, 128.16.32.15

c. 255.255.255.252, B,128.16.32.15, 128.16.32.12

d. 255.255.255.248, B,128.16.32.12, 128.16.32.15

3

TCP/IP ARCHITECTURE

Labs included in this chapter:

♦ Lab 3.1 Application Layer Protocols

♦ Lab 3.2 Transport Layer Protocols

♦ Lab 3.3 Internet Layer Protocols

♦ Lab 3.4 Network Interface Layer Protocols

Microsoft MCSE Exam #70-291 Objectives	
Objective	Lab
Manage DHCP.	3.1
Manage DNS.	3.1
Manage TCP/IP routing.	3.1, 3.3, 3.4
Troubleshoot connectivity to the Internet.	3.1, 3.2

LAB 3.1 APPLICATION LAYER PROTOCOLS

Objectives

The goal of this lab is to explore the application layer protocols in the TCP/IP model.

Materials Required

This lab will require the following:

- STUDENT1 Microsoft Windows Server 2003 access

- Internet access

- URLs of search engines recommended by your instructor (optional)

- List of search topics suggested by your instructor (optional)

Estimated completion time: **30 minutes**

Activity Background

As a networking administrator, you must become knowledgeable about the application layer protocols in the TCP/IP model. The application layer contains protocols that implement user-level functions, such as mail delivery, Web access, and file transfer. These applications are different from the user office applications like Microsoft Word or Excel.

HTTP (Hypertext Transfer Protocol) is a set of rules for exchanging files on the World Wide Web. Exchanged files include a wide range of media types: text, graphic images, sound, video, and other multimedia files. Your Web browser is an HTTP client, sending requests to HTTP Web servers.

FTP (File Transfer Protocol) is the simplest way to exchange files between nodes on the Internet. FTP is an application layer protocol that uses the Internet's TCP/IP protocols.

Telnet (Telephone Network) is the way you can access someone else's computer, assuming they have given you permission. With Telnet, you log on as a regular user with whatever privileges you may have been granted to the specific application and data on that computer.

SMTP (Simple Mail Transfer Protocol) is a TCP/IP protocol used in exchanging e-mail between servers. You typically use a mail client, such as Microsoft Outlook Express, that uses SMTP for sending e-mail to the user's mail server.

For retrieving messages stored at your local server, you can use Post Office Protocol version 3 (POP3) or Internet Message Access Protocol version 4 (IMAP4), which are also e-mail protocols.

IMAP4 is a standard protocol for accessing e-mail from your local server. IMAP is a client/server protocol in which your e-mail is received and held for you by your Internet server. You, using your e-mail client, can view just the heading and the sender of the letter and then decide whether to download the mail.

The DNS (Domain Name System) is the way that Internet domain names are located and translated into IP addresses. A domain name is meaningful and easier to remember than an IP address.

3

DHCP (Dynamic Host Configuration Protocol) is a protocol that lets you manage and automate the assignment of Internet Protocol (IP) addresses to the computers in your network.

In addition to an IP address, DHCP can provide IP configuration parameters: subnet masks, gateway IP addresses, and DNS IP addresses. DHCP uses the concept of a "lease," which is the amount of time that a given IP address will be valid for a computer.

ACTIVITY

Activity

1. Write a description of the application layer for the TCP/IP model.

_____

_____

_____

_____

_____

_____

2. Match the TCP/IP protocol with the task that the protocol could perform within the TCP/IP model.

TCP/IP Protocol	TCP/IP Task
1. DHCP ____	a. Resolve host names to IP addresses
2. DNS ____	b. Exchange WWW information
3. FTP ____	c. Access e-mail from local server
4. HTTP ____	d. Download e-mail to your server
5. IMAP4 ____	e. Run commands on another computer
6. POP3 ____	f. Provide IP configurations
7. SMTP ____	g. Download a file
8. Telnet ____	h. Transfer e-mail between servers

3. Log on to the **STUDENT1** server as **Administrator** with the password **secret**.

4. To start the Internet Explorer, click **Start**, point to **All Programs**, and click **Internet Explorer**.

5. If you receive a message indicating the Internet Explorer Enhanced Security Configuration setting is enabled on your server, click **OK** in the message box, click **Start**, click **Control Panel**, click **Add or Remove Programs**, click **Add/Remove Windows Components**, clear the **Internet Explorer Enhanced Security Configuration** check box, click the **Next** button, and then click the **Finish** button. Close Internet Explorer to apply the changes. Close the Add or Remove Programs window. Repeat Step 4.

NOTE

If a search engine is not available for your default web page, type *www.google.com* (or a search engine recommended by your instructor) in the Address bar, and then press Enter.

6. To search for information on the HTTP Application layer protocol, type **HTTP defined** in the Search text box, and then click **Search**.

7. To read an article, click its link that appears in Internet Explorer.

8. Record any relative information about the protocol, and then when you are done reading the article, click the **Back** button.

9. Read any additional articles that you think will be informative.

10. To view additional search entries, click the **Next** button located at the bottom of the window.

11. Repeat Steps 6 through 10 to search for information about the other application layer protocols.

12. Remain logged on to the STUDENT1 server for the next lab with the Internet Explorer open.

Certification Objectives

Objectives for MCSE Exam #70-291: Implementing, Managing, and Maintaining a Microsoft Windows Server 2003 Network:

- Manage DHCP.

- Manage DNS.

- Manage TCP/IP routing.

- Troubleshoot connectivity to the Internet.

REVIEW QUESTIONS

1. You are the network administrator for a chain of seafood restaurants. You are using Windows 2003 operating systems at each remote location. A bonus for making the trip to a remote store is the free seafood lunch. After lunch, you decide to connect to one of the remote UNIX computers at the home office to check the directory structure of the application directory. Which program will you start on the local computer?

    a. FTP

    b. SMTP

    c. ARP

    d. Telnet

    e. DNS

2. Continuing with your session at the remote restaurant, you decide that you want to transfer a file from the UNIX server. Which program will you use?

    a. FTP

    b. SMTP

    c. ARP

    d. Telnet

    e. DNS

3. You are aware that there are a number of e-mail applications available for the TCP/IP protocol suite. Which of the items below correctly identify the actions that the SMTP, IMAP4, and POP3 e-mail programs perform? (Choose all that apply.)

    a. SMTP moves e-mail from the server to your workstation.

    b. SMTP moves e-mail from your workstation to the server.

    c. IMAP4 holds e-mail on the server where you can read the e-mail from multiple workstations.

    d. IMAP4 requires that the e-mail be moved from the server to the workstation prior to reading the subject lines.

    e. POP3 holds e-mail on the server where you can read the e-mail from multiple workstations.

    f. POP3 requires that the e-mail be moved from the server to the workstation prior to reading the subject lines.

4. Mike and Lillie are discussing the advantages of using DHCP on a Windows 2003 network, and you join the discussion. Which of the items will you want to include as a list of characteristics of IP addressing in a Windows 2003 network? (Choose all that apply.)

   a. Host computers require IP addresses to communicate with other computers using the TCP/IP protocol suite.

   b. Without DHCP, administrators must enter IP address configurations manually.

   c. With DHCP, IP addresses are provided automatically.

   d. DHCP can provide subnet masks to the hosts.

   e. DHCP IP configurations are provided once and for the life of the host computer.

5. Which of the following TCP/IP protocols provides a method of exchanging text, graphic, sound, and video to the Internet Explorer?

   a. FTP

   b. DNS

   c. SMTP

   d. HTTP

   e. WWW

LAB 3.2 TRANSPORT LAYER PROTOCOLS

Objectives

The goal of this lab is to explore the transport layer protocols for the TCP/IP model.

Materials Required

This lab will require the following:

- STUDENT1 Microsoft Windows 2003 member server access

- Internet access

- URLs of search engines recommended by your instructor (optional)

- List of search topics suggested by your instructor (optional)

Estimated completion time: **30 minutes**

Activity Background

As a networking administrator, you must become knowledgeable about the transport layer protocols in the TCP/IP model. The transport layer handles connection setup, flow control, retransmission of lost data, and other generic data flow management. The mutually exclusive TCP and UDP protocols are this layer's most important members.

3

ACTIVITY

Activity

1. Write a description of the transport layer for the TCP/IP model.

_____

_____

_____

_____

_____

_____

_____

2. Make sure you are logged on to the STUDENT1 server and Internet Explorer is open.

3. To search for information on the TCP Transport layer protocol, type **TCP defined** in the Search text box, and then click **Search**.

4. To read an article, click its link that appears in Internet Explorer.

5. Record any relative information about the protocol, and when you are done reading the article, click the **Back** button.

6. Read any additional articles that you think will be informative.

7. To view additional search entries, click the **Next** button located at the bottom of the window.

8. To search for articles about the UDP protocol, repeat Steps 3 through 7 for **UDP defined**.

9. Remain logged on to the STUDENT1 server for the next lab with Internet Explorer open.

Certification Objectives

Objectives for MCSE Exam #70-291: Implementing, Managing, and Maintaining a Microsoft Windows Server 2003 Network:

■ Troubleshoot connectivity to the Internet.

REVIEW QUESTIONS

1. Which of the following tasks occur at the transport layer of the TCP/IP model? (Choose all that apply.)

   a. Support of user logon and authentication

   b. Rerouting of lost data when network segments are not available

   c. Flow control that regulates the speed at which packets arrive

   d. Reassembly of segmented packets

   e. Requiring the application program to ensure that the entire message has arrived

2. Which of the following characteristics are correct for the TCP protocol? (Choose all that apply.)

   a. Connection is established before data is transferred.

   b. Connection is not required before each datagram is transferred.

   c. Divides large packets into segments.

   d. Application program divides packets into segments.

   e. Receiving host acknowledges that the packets have arrived.

   f. Application program acknowledges that the datagrams have arrived.

3. Which of the following characteristics are correct for the UDP protocol? (Choose all that apply.)

   a. Connection is established before data is transferred.

   b. Connection is not required before each datagram is transferred.

   c. Divides large packets into segments.

   d. Application program divides packets into segments.

   e. Receiving host acknowledges that the packets have arrived.

   f. Application program acknowledges that the datagrams have arrived.

4. Which of the following are differences between the TCP and UDP transport protocols? (Choose all that apply.)

   a. TCP is reliable.

   b. UDP is reliable.

   c. TCP does not require connections.

   d. UDP does not require connections.

   e. UDP provides "best effort" communications.

   f. TCP provides "best effort" communications.

LAB 3.3 INTERNET LAYER PROTOCOLS

Objectives

The goal of this lab is to explore the Internet layer protocols for the TCP/IP model.

Materials Required

This lab will require the following:

- STUDENT1 Microsoft Windows Server 2003 member access

- Internet access

- URLs of search engines recommended by your instructor (optional)

- List of search topics suggested by your instructor (optional)

Estimated completion time: **30 minutes**

Activity Background

As a networking administrator, you must become knowledgeable about the Internet layer protocols in the TCP/IP model. The Internet layer is responsible for delivering data across a series of different physical networks that interconnect a source and destination node. Routing protocols are most closely associated with this layer, as is the IP Protocol, the Internet's fundamental protocol.

IP is the network layer protocol by which data is sent from one node to another on the Internet. Each node (known as a host) on the Internet has at least one IP address that uniquely identifies it from all other nodes on the Internet. IP is a connectionless protocol, which means that there is no continuing connection between the nodes that are communicating. Each packet that travels through the Internet is treated as an independent unit of data without any relation to any other unit of data. IP is also called an unreliable protocol. It is said that IP makes a "best effort" attempt to route the packet to the destination node but does not guarantee delivery.

The most widely used version of IP today is IP version 4 (IPv4). However, IP version 6 (IPv6) is also beginning to be supported. IPv6 provides for much longer addresses and provides additional routing capabilities.

ARP (Address Resolution Protocol) is a protocol for mapping an IP address to a MAC address that is recognized in the local network.

ICMP (Internet Control Message Protocol) is a message control and error-reporting protocol between a router and a host node.

Ping (Packet Internet Groper) is a basic troubleshooting program that lets you verify that a particular IP address exists and can accept requests. You use ping to ensure that a host computer you are trying to reach is actually operating. Tracert (trace route) is a utility that records the route (the specific routers at each hop) through the Internet between your computer and a specified destination computer.

IGMP (Internet Group Management Protocol) provides a way for an Internet computer to send its multicast group membership to adjacent routers. Multicasting allows one computer on the Internet to send content to multiple other computers that have identified themselves as interested in receiving the originating computer's content.

Routing Information Protocol (RIP) is a widely used protocol for managing router information within a self-contained network, such as a corporate local area network.

Using RIP, a gateway router sends its entire routing table (which lists all the other routers it knows about) to its closest neighbor router every 30 seconds. The neighbor router in turn will pass the information on to its next neighbor, and so on, until all routers within the network have the same knowledge of routing paths, a state known as network convergence.

Open Shortest Path First (OSPF) is a router protocol used within larger system networks in preference to RIP. Like RIP, OSPF is designated by the Internet Engineering Task Force (IETF) as one of several interior gateway protocols.

Using OSPF, a router that obtains a change to a routing table or detects a change in the network immediately multicasts the information to all other routers in the network so that all will have the same routing table information. Unlike the RIP in which the entire routing table is sent, the router using OSPF sends only the part that has changed. OSPF multicasts the updated information only when a change has taken place.

Activity

1. Write a description of the Internet layer for the TCP/IP model.

_____

_____

_____

_____

_____

_____

3

2. Match the TCP/IP Internet layer protocol with the task that the protocol could perform within the TCP/IP model.

TCP/IP Internet Layer Protocol	TCP/IP Task
1. ARP _____	a. Error-reporting
2. ICMP _____	b. Routing over large networks
3. IGMP _____	c. Sending data between nodes
4. IP _____	d. Routing over small networks
5. OSPF _____	e. Multicasting
6. RIP _____	f. Mapping IP addresses to MAC addresses

3. Verify that you are logged on to the STUDENT1 server with Internet Explorer open.

4. To search for information on the Internet layer protocol, type **Internet Protocol defined** in the Search text box, and then click **Search**.

5. To read an article, click the link that appears in Internet Explorer.

6. Record any relative information, and when you are done reading the article, click the **Back** button.

7. Read any additional articles that you think will be informative.

8. To view additional search entries, click the **Next** button located at the bottom of the window.

9. Repeat Steps 4 through 8 for additional topics.

10. Minimize Internet Explorer.

11. To open the command prompt window, click **Start**, and then click **Command Prompt**.

12. To test connectivity between the computers, type **ping 192.168.1.12** at the command prompt, and then press **Enter**.

13. To view the contents of the ARP cache, type **ARP –a** at the command prompt.

14. Close the command prompt window, and then restore Internet Explorer.

15. Remain logged on to the STUDENT1 server for the next lab with Internet Explorer open.

Certification Objectives

Objectives for MCSE Exam #70-291: Implementing, Managing, and Maintaining a Microsoft Windows Server 2003 Network:

■ Manage TCP/IP routing.

REVIEW QUESTIONS

1. Which of the following items would you include in a discussion of the IP protocol? (Choose all that apply.)

   a. No continuing connection is needed between computers to exchange packets.

   b. Each packet travels through the Internet unaware of any previous or successive packets.

   c. A "best effort" attempt is made to deliver the packet.

   d. IP depends on TCP to provide reliability.

   e. Although version 4 is the current version, the Internet will move to version 5 soon.

2. You know from your Internet study that ARP is the Address Resolution Protocol. You want to make sure that your notes on ARP are correct. You ask Kellie to look over your notes. Which of the following statements is true about ARP? (Choose all that apply.)

   a. ARP uses broadcasts to locate the host with the correct IP address.

   b. ARP checks the ARP cache to see if a host has previously exchanged frames.

   c. The ARP cache contains host names, IP addresses, and MAC addresses.

   d. ARP determines the IP address for a MAC address.

   e. ARP determines the MAC address for the IP address.

3. There are two prevalent IP protocols that use ICMP Echo Requests and Echo Replies. Which of the following tasks can these protocols perform? (Choose all that apply.)

    a. Connecting to a computer to execute commands with ping

    b. Checking connectivity to a remote computer with ping

    c. Checking connectivity to a remote computer with tracert

    d. Determining the path that a packet takes through the Internet with tracert

    e. Transferring files through the Internet with Telnet

4. Which of the following are correct statements about IGPs? (Choose all that apply.)

    a. Because RIP updates routing tables every 30 seconds, RIP is an excellent solution for large scale networks.

    b. Because OSPF uses link state updates, convergence is a problem.

    c. RIP uses the number of hops to assess the desirability of a given network link.

    d. OSPF uses cost metrics to determine which route to take.

    e. Because OSPF uses multicasts to exchange routing updates, OSPF is more efficient than RIP.

Lab 3.4 Network Interface Layer Protocols

Objectives

The goal of this lab is to explore the network interface layer protocols of the TCP/IP model.

Materials Required

This lab will require the following:

- STUDENT1 Microsoft Windows Server 2003 member access

- Internet access

- URLs of search engines recommended by your instructor (optional)

- List of search topics suggested by your instructor (optional)

Estimated completion time: **30 minutes**

Activity Background

As a networking administrator, you must become knowledgeable about the network interface layer protocols in the TCP/IP model. The network interface layer is responsible for delivering data over the particular hardware media in use. Different protocols are selected from this layer, depending on the type of physical network. Recall that the DOD did not specify protocols at this layer. It wanted to leave this layer open in an attempt to encourage vendors to include its network interface protocols.

Recall that the network interface layer is the equivalent of the OSI physical and data link layers because it defines the host's connection to the network. This layer comprises the hardware and software involved in the interchange of frames between computers. The technologies used can be either LAN-based or WAN-based.

The LAN-based protocols that you may encounter as a network administrator are:

- Ethernet—most common LAN technology

- Token Ring—common to organizations employing IBM mainframe computers

- FDDI—used with geographically dispersed networks

- AppleTalk—originally created for Apple computers

The WAN-based protocols that you may encounter as a network administrator are:

- SLIP (Serial Line Internet Protocol)—predecessor to PPP

- PPP (Point-to-Point Protocol)—preferred dial-up protocol

- High-level Data Link Control (HDLC)—widely used to connect between network points

- ATM (Asynchronous Transfer Mode)—dedicated-connection switching technology that organizes digital data into 53-byte cell units

- X.25—predecessor to frame relay

- Frame relay—designed for cost-efficient data transmission for intermittent traffic between local area networks

Activity

1. Write a description of the network interface layer for the TCP/IP model.

_____

_____

_____

_____

_____

2. Match the LAN network interface layer protocol with the probable use.

TCP/IP LAN Protocol	Network Interface Property
1. AppleTalk ____	a. IBM mainframes
2. Ethernet ____	b. Apple computers
3. FDDI ____	c. Longer LAN connections
4. Token Ring ____	d. Most common LAN

3. Match the WAN network interface layer protocol with the characteristic.

TCP/IP WAN Protocol	Network Interface Characteristic
1. ATM ____	a. Predecessor to frame relay
2. Frame relay ____	b. Widely used between network points
3. HDLC ____	c. Dedicated-switching with digital data
4. PPP ____	d. Predecessor to PPP
5. SLIP ____	e. Used by Internet service providers
6. X.25 ____	f. Traffic between LANs

4. Verify that you are logged on to the STUDENT1 server and Internet Explorer is open.

5. To search for information on the Ethernet network interface layer protocol, type **Ethernet defined** in the Search text box, and then click **Search**.

6. To read an article, click the link that appears in Internet Explorer.

7. Record any relative information, and then when you're done reading the article, click the **Back** button.

8. Read any additional articles that you think will be informative.

9. To view additional search entries, click the **Next** button located at the bottom of the window.

10. Repeat Steps 5 through 9 for the remaining topics.

11. Close Internet Explorer and then log off the STUDENT1 server.

Certification Objectives

Objectives for MCSE Exam #70-291: Implementing, Managing, and Maintaining a Microsoft Windows Server 2003 Network:

- Manage TCP/IP routing.

REVIEW QUESTIONS

1. You start your study for the next quiz by writing down significant facts regarding the LAN/WAN protocols used in networks. Which of the following statements are true about LAN/WAN protocols? (Choose all that apply.)

   a. The OSI physical and datalink layers are equivalent to this layer.

   b. The protocol is comprised of hardware and software to move frames of data.

   c. Technologies can be LAN-based.

   d. Technologies can be WAN-based.

   e. The DOD did not specify protocols at this layer.

2. You are designing a complex network that requires multiple protocols. Which of the following statements will you include in your proposal? (Choose all that apply.)

   a. Ethernet enjoys great popularity as a network interface protocol.

   b. Since our network supports an IBM mainframe, token ring should be considered.

   c. FDDI's extended length makes it an ideal candidate for the backbone.

   d. HDLC could be used to provide high-speed connections to remote offices.

   e. Frame relay could be used to provide intermittent connections to smaller remote offices.

3. You are considering a dial-up protocol for your remote offices. Which of the following should you use?

   a. SLIP

   b. PPP

   c. HDLC

   d. ATM

   e. Frame relay

4. You need to select a WAN protocol for light, infrequent connections usage by your remote offices. You will need to connect at a minimum transmission speed of 256 Mbps. Which of the following should you use?

   a. SLIP

   b. PPP

   c. HDLC

   d. ATM

   e. Frame relay

5. You need to select a WAN protocol that will permit the transmission of voice, video, and digital data over digital connections. Which WAN protocol will you communication provider suggest?

   a. SLIP

   b. PPP

   c. HDLC

   d. ATM

   e. Frame relay

3

IMPLEMENTING DYNAMIC HOST CONFIGURATION PROTOCOL (DHCP)

Labs included in this chapter:

♦ Lab 4.1 Installing Active Directory

♦ Lab 4.2 Adding and Authorizing a DHCP Server Service

♦ Lab 4.3 Creating DHCP Scopes

♦ Lab 4.4 Creating Reservations

♦ Lab 4.5 Configuring a DHCP Relay Agent

Microsoft Exam #70-291 Objectives	
Objective	Lab
Manage DHCP	4.1, 4.2, 4.3, 4.4, 4.5
Troubleshoot TCP/IP Addressing	4.3, 4.4, 4.5
Troubleshoot DHCP	4.2, 4.3, 4.4, 4.5

LAB 4.1 INSTALLING ACTIVE DIRECTORY

Objectives

The goal of this lab is to install Active Directory.

Materials Required

The lab will require the following:

- The STUDENT1 server, as described in the lab setup section in the front of this lab manual

- Microsoft Windows Server 2003 CD-ROM

> Estimated completion time: **30 minutes**

Activity Background

Active Directory is the directory service for Windows 2003 networking and is required for a proper installation of the Dynamic Host Configuration Protocol (DHCP). DHCP is tightly integrated with Domain Name System (DNS), Routing and Remote Access Service (RRAS), and Active Directory. The installation of DHCP requires Active Directory and DNS.

ACTIVITY

Activity

1. Logon to the STUDENT1 computer as **administrator** with the password **secret**.

2. Insert the Windows Server 2003 CD-ROM into the appropriate drive. If the Welcome screen appears, click the **Exit** hyperlink to close it.

3. To display the Internet Protocol (TCP/IP) Properties dialog box, click **Start**, point to **Control Panel**, point to **Network Connections**, click **Local Area Connection**, click the **Properties** button, click **Internet Protocol (TCP/IP)**, and then click the **Properties** button.

4. To configure TCP/IP for the STUDENT1 server, click the **Use the following IP address** radio button, type **192.168.1.1** in the IP address text box, press the **Tab** key and confirm that **255.255.255.0** appears in the Subnet mask text box, type **192.168.1.1** in the Preferred DNS server text box, click the **OK** button, and then click the **Close** button twice.

5. To disable the second network card, click **Start**, point to **Control Panel**, point to **Network Connections**, right-click **Local Area Connection 2**, click **Disable**, and then click in a blank area of the desktop to close the Start menu.

6. To launch the Active Directory Installation Wizard, click **Start**, click **Run**, type **dcpromo** in the **Open** text box, and then click the **OK** button.

7. To install Active Directory, click the **Next** button twice, verify that the **Domain controller for a new domain** radio button is selected, click the **Next** button, verify that the **Domain in a new forest** radio button is selected, and then click the **Next** button.

8. To specify the DNS name, type **domain1.classroom.com** in the Full DNS name for new domain text box, click **Next**, verify that **DOMAIN1** is contained in the Domain NetBIOS name text box, and then click the **Next** button three times to accept the default file locations.

9. To install DNS, verify that the **Install and configure the DNS server on this computer** radio button is selected, click the **Next** button, verify that the **Permissions compatible only with Windows 2000 or Windows Server 2003 operating systems** radio button is selected, and then click the **Next** button.

10. To specify the Directory Services Restore Mode Administrator Password, type **Secret1** in the Restore Mode Password text box, press the **Tab** key, type **Secret1** in the Confirm password text box, and then click the **Next** button.

11. Review the Summary, and then click the **Next** button.

12. Wait for the wizard to complete the Active Directory configuration.

13. Click the **Finish** button, close any open applications, and then click the **Restart Now** button.

Certification Objectives

Objectives for Microsoft Exam #70-291: Implementing, Managing, and Maintaining a Microsoft Windows Server 2003 Network Infrastructure:

- Manage DHCP

REVIEW QUESTIONS

1. You plan to install DHCP services for your new Windows 2003 network. You recall that you must install Active Directory to authorize your DHCP server to issue IP addresses to the DHCP clients on your network. Which items will you need to specify for the installation of Active Directory for your new Windows 2003 network? (Choose all that apply.)

   a. domain called forest.com

   b. a tree called pine

   c. a forest called northern

   d. an administrator password

   e. an IP address of 192.168.33.1

   f. a subnet mask of 255.255.255.0

2. Ashley and Chrissy discuss rogue DHCP servers. They ask you for clarification on the impact of rogue DHCP servers on a Windows 2003 network. Which of the following will you include in your discussion? (Choose all that apply.)

   a. They lease incorrect IP addresses to clients.

   b. They provide incorrect subnet masks to clients.

   c. They provide correct subnet masks to clients.

   d. They lease correct IP addresses to clients.

   e. They lease duplicate IP addresses to clients.

3. When using DHCP in a Windows 2003 network, DHCP services can be integrated with numerous network services. Which of the following are frequently integrated with DHCP? (Choose all that apply.)

   a. DNS

   b. RRAS

   c. AD

   d. WINS

   e. WANS

LAB 4.2 ADDING AND AUTHORIZING A DHCP SERVER SERVICE

Objectives

The goal of this lab is to install the DHCP Service.

Materials Required

The lab will require the following:

- The STUDENT1 server, as described in the lab setup section in the front of this lab manual

- Completion of Lab 4.1

Estimated completion time: **10 minutes**

Activity Background

Network administrators use DHCP servers to manage dynamic allocation of IP addresses and other related configuration details to DHCP-enabled clients on the network.

 Activity

1. Logon to the STUDENT1 computer as **administrator** with the password **secret**.

2. To launch the Windows Server 2003 Configure Your Server Wizard, click **Start**, point to **Administrative Tools**, and then click **Configure Your Server Wizard**.

3. When the Welcome to the Configure Your Server Wizard window appears, click the **Next** button.

4. Review the Preliminary Steps and then click the **Next** button.

5. To install the DHCP service, click **DHCP server** in the Server Role list, and then click the **Next** button.

6. Review the Summary of Selections and then click the **Next** button.

7. When the Configuring components window appears, wait for the DHCP service to be configured.

8. When the Welcome to the New Scope Wizard appears, click the **Cancel** button, and then click the **Finish** button.

9. To access the DHCP service console, click **Start**, point to **Administrative Tools**, and then click **DHCP**.

10. To authorize the DHCP Service, click **DHCP** at the root of the console tree, click the **Action** menu, click **Manage authorized servers**, click the **Authorize** button, type **192.168.1.1** in the Name or IP address text box, click the **OK** button twice, and then click the **Close** button.

11. To refresh the DHCP console window, click **student1.domain1.classroom.com** in the console tree, and then click the **Refresh** button (the button resembles a sheet of paper with two arrows), or press the **F5** key to refresh. Verify that the **student1.domain1.classroom.com** server has a green arrow.

12. To display the Server Properties page, click **student1.domain1.classroom.com** in the console tree, click the **Action** menu, and then click **Properties**.

13. Review the information on the General tab, DNS tab, and the Advanced tab, and then click the **Cancel** button to close.

14. Remain logged onto the STUDENT1 server with the DHCP console open.

Certification Objectives

Objectives for Microsoft Exam #70-291: Implementing, Managing, and Maintaining a Microsoft Windows Server 2003 Network Infrastructure:

- Manage DHCP

- Troubleshoot DHCP

REVIEW QUESTIONS

1. After the client chooses to accept the IP lease offer, how does the DHCP client respond to the DHCP server?

   a. DHCPOFFER

   b. DHCPACK

   c. DHCPREQUEST

   d. DHCPDISCOVER

   e. DHCPSELECTION

2. After the DHCP server is notified that it will be providing the IP lease, how does the DHCP server provide the additional IP configuration to the DHCP client?

   a. DHCPOFFER

   b. DHCPACK

   c. DHCPREQUEST

   d. DHCPDISCOVER

   e. DHCPSELECTION

3. Your Windows 2003 network has an existing Windows Server 2003 with Active Directory. You install the DHCP service on a standalone Windows Server 2003. What will be your next task to authorize the new DHCP server?

   a. Run the Authorize DHCP Servers Wizard.

   b. Use Active Directory Users and Computers to authorize the server.

   c. Use Active Directory Sites and Services to authorize the server.

   d. This server can not be authorized.

   e. Use the DHCP console to authorize the server.

4. Lillie and Mike discuss unauthorized, or rogue, DHCP servers. They ask you for the steps that DHCP servers take to ensure that the server is not a rogue. Which of the following will you tell Lillie and Mike? (Choose all that apply.)

   a. The Active Directory contains a list of authorized servers.

   b. The domain controller contains a list of authorized servers.

   c. When starting up, the DHCP server queries the domain controller.

   d. When starting up, the DHCP server queries the Active Directory.

   e. If a match is found, the server is identified as authorized.

   f. If a match is not found, the server is identified as authorized.

   g. If authorized, the server is automatically shutdown.

5. You are going to install and authorize DHCP services in your server lab today. You ponder this question as you walk to class today. How will you know that DHCP has been authorized?

   a. The refresh button works.

   b. The server entry says Authorized.

   c. The arrow is green next to the server icon.

   d. DHCP is indicated as authorized in Active Directory.

Lab 4.3 Creating DHCP Scopes

Objectives

The goal of this lab is to create a DHCP address scope for an existing DHCP server.

Materials Required

The lab will require the following:

- The STUDENT1 server, as described in the lab setup section in the front of this lab manual

- Completion of Labs 4.1 and 4.2

Estimated completion time: **20 minutes**

Activity Background

You create a DHCP address scope for each physical subnet and then use the scope to define the configuration parameters used by clients. Without a scope, the DHCP service will not be able to provide configuration for the DHCP clients.

Activity

ACTIVITY

1. Remain logged on to the STUDENT1 computer with the DHCP console open.

2. To start the New Scope Wizard, click **student1.domain1.classroom.com** in the DHCP console tree, click the **Action** menu, and then click **New Scope**.

3. To provide the scope name, click **Next**, and then type **Team01** in the Name text box.

4. To enter the IP address range and subnet mask, click **Next**, type **192.168.1.1** in the Start IP address text box, press the **Tab** key, type **192.168.1.200** in the End IP address text box, press the **Tab** key, verify that **255.255.255.0** is listed in the Subnet mask text box, and then click the **Next** button.

5. To enter IP address exclusion for the two servers, type **192.168.1.1** in the Start IP address text box, press the **Tab** key, type **192.168.1.2** in the End IP address text box, click the **Add** button, and then click the **Next** button.

6. To set the lease duration to 1 hour, type **0** in the Days text box, type **1** in the Hours text box, and then click the **Next** button.

7. To configure the DHCP options later, click the **No, I will configure these options later** radio button, click the **Next** button, and then click the **Finish** button.

8. To activate the DHCP scope, click **Scope [192.168.1.0] Team01** in the console tree, click the **Action** menu, and then click **Activate**.

9. Click the **Refresh** icon (the icon resembles a sheet of paper with two arrows), or press the **F5** key to refresh. Verify that the **student1.domain1.classroom.com** server has a green arrow.

10. To launch the New Superscope Wizard, click **student1.domain1.classroom.com** in the console tree, click the **Action** menu, click **New Superscope**, click the **Next** button, type **110superscope** in Name text box, click the **Next** button, click **[192.168.1.0] Team01** in the Available scopes list, click the **Next** button, review the superscope info, and then click the **Finish** button.

11. To create a new scope, click **student1.domain1.classroom.com** in the console tree, click the **Action** menu, click **New Scope**, click the **Next** button, type **Team01** in the Name text box, click **Next**, type **192.168.110.1** in the Start IP address text box, press the **Tab** key, type **192.168.110.254** in the End IP address text box, click the **Next** button twice, type **0** in the Days text box, type **1** in the Hours text box, click the **Next** button, click the **No, I will configure these options later** radio button, click the **Next** button, and then click the **Finish** button.

12. To activate the scope, click **Scope [192.168.110.0] Team01** in the console tree, click the **Action** menu, and then click **Activate**.

13. To add the new scope to a superscope, click **Scope [192.168.110.0] Team01** in the console tree, click the **Action** menu, click **Add To Superscope**, click **110superscope** in the Available superscopes list, and then click the **OK** button.

14. To create a new multicast scope, click **student1.domain1.classroom.com** in the console tree, click the **Action** menu, click **New Multicast Scope**, click the **Next** button, type **Multicast Team01** in the Name text box, click **Next**, type **239.192.0.0** in the Start IP address text box, press the **Tab** key, type **239.192.1.0** in the End IP address text box, verify that the TTL is set to the default of **32**, click the **Next** button twice, verify that the lease is set to **30** days, click the **Next** button twice, and then click the **Finish** button.

TIP   The status states ****Active**** in the right pane of the DHCP console for active superscopes and multicast scopes.

15. Remain logged on to the STUDENT1 server with the DHCP console window open.

Certification Objectives

Objectives for Microsoft Exam #70-291: Implementing, Managing, and Maintaining a Microsoft Windows Server 2003 Network Infrastructure:

- Manage DHCP

- Troubleshoot DHCP

- Troubleshoot TCP/IP Addressing

REVIEW QUESTIONS

1. When do DHCP clients attempt to contact the DHCP server that provided the lease to renew their existing lease for the first time?

   a. When 25% of the lease duration has expired?

   b. When 87.5% of the lease duration has expired?

   c. When 50% of the lease duration has expired?

   d. When 75% of the lease duration has expired?

2. Your company has used static IP addresses for the computers on the network. As the company has grown, additional networks have been allocated additional IP address ranges. Being a new employee, you questioned why static IP addresses were being used. You were informed that the previous network designer did not want a single point of failure. You are aware that redundancy can be provided by using multiple DHCP servers. Which of the following possible scope configurations will you select? (Choose all that apply.)

   a. DHCPSRV01: Scope A 192.168.22.1 to 192.168.22.250

   b. DHCPSRV02: Scope B 192.168.23.1 to 192.168.23.250

   c. DHCPSRV01: Scope A 192.168.22.1 to 192.168.22.200 Scope B 192.168.23.1 to 192.168.23.200

   d. DHCPSRV02: Scope A 192.168.22.51 to 192.168.22.250 Scope B 192.168.23.51 to 192.168.23.250

   e. DHCPSRV01: Scope A 192.168.22.1 to 192.168.22.50 Scope B 192.168.23.51 to 192.168.23.250

   f. DHCPSRV02: Scope A 192.168.22.51 to 192.168.22.250 Scope B 192.168.23.1 to 192.168.23.50

3. Your shop has used static IP addresses since the "turn of the century." You would like to bring your network up to the current year. You are aware that all of the servers and routers are assigned the low IP address range. However, your boss is reluctant to allow you to make the change because he is afraid that DHCP might assign IP addresses that duplicate the static IP addresses assigned to servers. How will you configure DHCP to minimize the possibility of a client computer duplicating an address assigned to a server? (Choose all that apply.)

   a. IP address range 192.168.1.1 – 192.168.1.254 assigned to the scope

   b. IP address range 192.168.1.1 – 192.168.1.254 assigned to the server

   c. IP address range 192.168.1.1 – 192.168.1.24 assigned to the exclusions

   d. IP address range 192.168.1.25 – 192.168.1.254 assigned to the clients

   e. IP address range 192.168.1.1 – 192.168.1.24 assigned to the reservations

4. Betty asks Bob for a clarification on superscopes. She has listed the following information about superscopes. Which of the following will Bob indicate are correct?

   a. Superscopes permit an administrator to group multiple scopes into a single administrative entity.

   b. Superscopes permit the creation of Class E IP addresses.

   c. With superscopes, you can overlap existing scopes without IP address conflicts.

   d. Enable the use of two DHCP servers on a single physical network.

5. Betty and Bob continue their discussion on DHCP scopes. Bob asks Betty about multicast scopes. Which of the following will Betty indicate are correct? (Choose all that apply.)

   a. useful for delivery of infrmation to a group of computers

   b. another name for broadcasts

   c. group members can enter or leave at will

   d. may disturb nonlistening nodes

   e. use the 239.162.0.0 Organization Local Scope for in-house video

4

LAB 4.4 CREATING RESERVATIONS

Objectives

The goal of this lab is to create a DHCP address reservation for clients on an existing DHCP Server. The reservation contains the client's MAC address.

Materials Required

The lab will require the following:

- The STUDENT1 and STUDENT2 servers, as described in the lab setup section in the front of this lab manual

- Completion of Labs 4.1 through 4.3

Estimated completion time: **10 minutes**

Activity Background

When you reserve a DHCP address, the DHCP server always assigns the same IP address to the client. When DHCP is asked to provide an IP address, the client computer transfers its MAC address facilitating a lookup for the previously defined IP address reservation.

Activity

1. Logon to the STUDENT2 server.

2. Return to the STUDENT1 server with the DHCP console window open.

3. To view the MAC address of the STUDENT2 server, click **Start**, click **Command Prompt**, type **nbtstat –a STUDENT2** at the command prompt, and then press the **Enter** key.

4. Record the MAC address for use in Step 5 and then close the Command Prompt window.

5. To display the Reservation dialog box in the DHCP console, expand **Scope [192.168.1.0] Team01**, expand the **Reservations** folder, right-click **Reservations**, and then click **New Reservation**.

6. To complete the reservation, type **Reservation for Student2** in the Reservation name text box, confirm that **192.168.1.** is in the IP address text box, type **2** to complete the IP address, type the MAC address recorded in Step 3 without the hyphens in the MAC address text box, click the **Add** button, and then click the **Close** button.

The reserved IP address must be within the valid dynamic range of addresses available in the scope.

NOTE

7. Remain logged on to the STUDENT1 server with the DHCP console open.

Certification Objectives

Objectives for Microsoft Exam #70-291: Implementing, Managing, and Maintaining a Microsoft Windows Server 2003 Network Infrastructure:

- Manage DHCP

- Troubleshoot DHCP

- Troubleshoot TCP/IP Addressing

REVIEW QUESTIONS

1. You are discussing DHCP reservations with your study group. During a break in the discussion on DHCP reservations, Danielle asks how to get a MAC address for a NIC card. What do you tell Danielle? (Choose all that apply.)

    a. Use the ipconfig /all command.

    b. Use the NICaddr command.

    c. Use the nbstat –A command.

    d. Use the nbstat –a command.

    e. Use the netstat command.

2. You continue your discussion with the study group. Professor Boswell lectured on DHCP reservations. You want to be sure you have the steps down for a DHCP reservation. What are the correct steps in the correct sequence for an IP address reservation?

    a. DHCP client sends a message for an IP address and includes the MAC address.

    b. DHCP client requests a reservation.

    c. DHCP server looks up the MAC address in the DHCP database.

    d. DHCP server generates a random IP address.

    e. DHCP server responds with the IP address from the DHCP database.

3. User Joe has an application that requires a fixed IP address. Your boss has firmly stated that static IP addresses can be assigned only to servers and routers. How will you help Joe run his application?

    a. Use a pseudo IP address.

    b. Setup a router to do network address translation.

    c. Create an IP address reservation.

    d. Replace the burned-in address in the NIC with an IP address.

LAB 4.5 CONFIGURING A DHCP RELAY AGENT

Objectives

The goal of this lab is to create a DHCP relay agent for clients that cannot gain access to a DHCP Server.

Materials Required

The lab will require the following:

- The STUDENT2 server, as described in the lab setup section in the front of this lab manual

- Completion of Labs 4.1 through 4.4

Estimated completion time: **15 minutes**

Activity Background

A relay agent is a small program that relays DHCP messages between clients and servers on different subnets. Routers are normally configured to block the broadcast messages that are used in the DHCP process.

Activity

ACTIVITY

1. Return to the STUDENT2 server.

2. To open the Routing and Remote Access Services console, click **Start**, point to **Administrative Tools**, and then click **Routing and Remote Access**.

3. To start the Routing and Remote Access Configuration Wizard, right-click **STUDENT2** in the console tree, and then click on **Configure and Enable Routing and Remote Access**.

4. To specify LAN Routing and start Routing and Remote Access, click the **Next** button, click the **Custom configuration** radio button, click the **Next** button, click the **LAN routing** check box, click the **Next** button to review the Summary of selections list, click the **Finish** button, and then click the **Yes** button.

5. Wait until the Routing and Remote Access service starts.

6. To add the DHCP Relay Agent, expand **IP Routing** in the console tree, right-click **General**, click **New Routing Protocol**, click **DHCP Relay Agent**, and then click the **OK** button.

7. To configure the DHCP Relay Agent properties, right-click **DHCP Relay Agent**, click **Properties**, type **192.168.1.1** in the Server address text box, click the **Add** button, click the **Apply** button, and then click the **OK** button.

8. Close all open windows and then shut down the STUDENT2 server.

9. Return to the STUDENT1 server. Close all open windows and shut down the STUDENT1 server.

Certification Objectives

Objectives for Microsoft Exam #70-291: Implementing, Managing, and Maintaining a Microsoft Windows Server 2003 Network Infrastructure:

- Manage DHCP

- Troubleshoot DHCP

- Troubleshoot TCP/IP Addressing

REVIEW QUESTIONS

4

1. First, you install the DHCP Server service on a computer running Windows Server 2003 on subnetA. Next, you want client computers on subnetB to acquire addresses from the DHCP server in subnetA. You check the network diagram and discover that the router connects to both subnetA and subnetB. What utility program should you use to configure a computer running Windows Server 2003 on subnetB as a DHCP relay agent?

   a. Routing and Remote Access Service

   b. Properties dialog box of the Local Area Connection

   c. Registry Editor

   d. Add/Remove Programs

2. You install the DHCP Server service on a computer running Windows Server 2003 on subnetA. You want client computers on subnetB to acquire addresses from this DHCP server. SubnetA and subnetB are connected to the same router. What should you do to ensure that client computers on subnetB can receive IP addresses from the DHCP server on subnetA?

   a. Configure the DHCP client requestor on each client on subnetB to use the DHCP server on subnetA.

   b. Configure the DHCP relay service on a Windows Server 2003 on subnetB.

   c. Install a DHCP relay appliance on subnetB.

   d. There is no reason why the router will not forward the DHCP broadcast messages from subnetB to subnetA.

3. Use Figure 4-1 for this question.

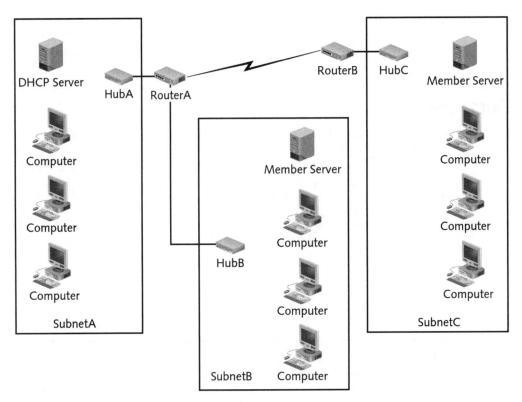

Figure 4-1   Three subnets requiring a Relay Agent

There are three subnets in the network with routers between the subnets. RouterB is a noncompliant router, which means it not capable of processing DHCP messages. Where will you place the DHCP Relay agent(s) to enable clients to obtain IP addresses? (Choose all that apply.)

a. Place the DHCP relay agents on the HubB and HubC.

b. Place the DHCP relay agents on the RouterB.

c. Place the DHCP relay agent on the DHCP server.

d. Place the DHCP relay agent on the member server on SubnetB.

e. Place the DHCP relay agent on the member server on SubnetC.

4. You are the network administrator for Life is Swell, Inc. Each segment has a number of clients and servers located on it, including an Active Directory server, a DNS server, and a DHCP server. Clients normally obtain addressing information from their local DHCP server. You want to enable users to be able to obtain addressing information from either DHCP server. The router is RFC1542 compliant. How can you accomplish this?

   a. Configure a server on each subnet to act as a DHCP Relay Agent. Point the Relay Agent to the DHCP server on the same subnet.

   b. Configure each DHCP server to use redactive scopes. Configure each with the other DHCP server as its partner.

   c. Configure a server on each subnet to act as a DHCP Relay Agent. Point the Relay Agent to the DHCP server on the other subnet.

   d. Configure each DHCP server to use shared scopes using the 80/20 rule. Configure each with the other DHCP server as its partner.

4

MANAGING AND MONITORING
DHCP

Labs included in this chapter:

♦ Lab 5.1 Backing Up and Restoring a DHCP Database

♦ Lab 5.2 Viewing Statistics

♦ Lab 5.3 DHCP Audit Logging

♦ Lab 5.4 Using Conflict Detection

♦ Lab 5.5 Viewing DHCP Events in Event Viewer

♦ Lab 5.6 Troubleshooting DHCP

Microsoft MCSE Exam #70-291 Objectives	
Objective	Lab
Manage DHCP	5.1, 5.2, 5.3, 5.4, 5.5
Troubleshoot DHCP	5.1, 5.2, 5.3, 5.4, 5.5, 5.6

Lab 5.1 Backing Up and Restoring a DHCP Database

Objectives

The primary goal of this lab is to back up and restore the DHCP database. A secondary goal is to perform offline DHCP database maintenance.

Materials Required

This lab will require the following:

- STUDENT1 server access

- Completion of Labs 4.1 through 4.5

Estimated completion time: **20 minutes**

Activity Background

As a network administrator, you will want to periodically backup the contents of your DHCP database. Restoring the DHCP server database can be useful in situations where the database has either become corrupted or lost.

ACTIVITY

Activity

1. Logon to the STUDENT1 server as **Administrator** with the password **secret**.

2. To access the DHCP service console, click **Start**, point to **Administrative Tools**, and then click **DHCP**.

3. To start the backup of the DHCP database, expand **student1.domain1.classroom.com [192.168.1.1]**, right-click **student1.domain1.classroom.com [192.168.1.1]**, click **Backup**, click the **backup** folder, and then click **OK**.

4. To restore the DHCP database, click **student1.domain1.classroom.com [192.168.1.1]**, right-click **student1.domain1.classroom.com [192.168.1.1]**, and then click **Restore**.

5. To specify the location of the back up files, expand the **backup** folder, click the **New** folder, and then click **OK**.

6. When the message is displayed to stop and start the DHCP service, click **Yes**.

7. Wait for the DHCP database to be restored.

8. To open a command prompt, click **Start**, and then click **Command Prompt**.

9. To stop the DHCP service, type **net stop dhcpserver** at the command prompt, and then press **Enter**. A message similar to the following appears:

```
C:\>net stop dhcpserver
The DHCP Server service is stopping.
The DHCP Server service was stopped successfully.
```

10. To position the current directory to the location of the DHCP database, type **cd \windows\system32\dhcp** at the command prompt, and then press **Enter**.

11. To compact the DHCP database, type **jetpack dhcp.mdb temp.mdb**, and then press **Enter**. A message similar to the following appears:

```
C:\WINDOWS\system32\dhcp>jetpack dhcp.mdb temp.mdb
Compacted database dhcp.mdb in 3.745 seconds.
moving temp.mdb => dhcp.mdb
jetpack completed successfully.
```

12. To start the DHCP service, type **net start dhcpserver** at the command prompt, and then press **Enter**. A message similar to the following appears:

```
C:\WINDOWS\system32\dhcp>net start dhcpserver
The DHCP Server service is starting...
The DHCP Server service was started successfully.
```

13. Close the command prompt window.

14. Remain logged onto the STUDENT1 server and leave the DHCP console open for the next lab.

Certification Objectives

Objectives for Microsoft Exam #70-291: Implementing, Managing, and Maintaining a Microsoft Windows Server 2003 Network Infrastructure:

- Manage DHCP

- Troubleshoot DHCP

REVIEW QUESTIONS

1. David needs to back up the DHCP database. He opens the DHCP window and notices in the right pane that the DHCP server is listed with a status of "Not connected." What does David need to do to correct the problem?

   a. Authorize the DHCP server in Active Directory.

   b. Start the DHCP service.

   c. Close the DHCP console and restart the DHCP console.

   d. Click the server name.

2. Rachel and Victor discuss the DHCP database, making the following statements about it. Which of the following statements about the DHCP database are true? (Choose all that apply.)

   a. The DHCP database is limited to 1,000 entries.

   b. The DHCP database grows as DHCP clients start and stop on the network.

   c. The DHCP server dynamically compacts the database during idle periods.

   d. For smaller networks, you should perform manual compaction weekly.

   e. The DHCP server must be stopped for compacting to be performed offline.

3. You are backing up the DHCP server in lab today. What is the correct order of the steps to back up a DHCP database?

   1 Stop the DHCP service.

   2 Specify the location of the back up folder.

   3 Start the DHCP service.

   4 Right-click the server name.

   5 Select Backup.

   a. 1, 4, 5, 2

   b. 4, 5, 2

   c. 1, 4, 5, 2, 3

   d. 1, 5, 4, 2, 3

4. You are the network administrator for Trucks=Fun, which is a company that specializes in off-road truck rentals. And yes, you receive discounted rentals every Tuesday. You have over 2000 hosts on your network. What commands should you issue to compact the DHCP database? (Choose all that apply.)

   a. Net stop dhcp

   b. Net stop dhcpserver

   c. Jetpack

   d. Jetpack dhcp.mdb temp.mdb

   e. Net start dhcp

   f. Net start dhcpserver

5. Your new server has arrived! You envision that your DHCP problems are going to rapidly disappear. You install Windows Server 2003 on the new computer. You want to use the DHCP database on the new server. What step(s) will you need to place the DHCP database from the former DHCP server on the new server?

   a. Use the DHCP console Move database option to move the database to the new machine.

   b. Back up the DHCP database, create a share for the backup folder, and copy the database to the new machine.

   c. Use the movedhcp program to move the database to the new computer.

   d. Remove the hard drive from the existing computer, and add the hard drive to the new computer as a foreign drive.

Lab 5.2 Viewing Statistics

Objectives

The goal of this lab is to view the DHCP statistics with the DHCP management console.

Materials Required

This lab will require the following:

- STUDENT1 server access

- Completion of Lab 5.1

Estimated completion time:	**15 minutes**

Activity Background

The DHCP statistics include the total number of scopes and addresses on the server, the number used, and the number available. These statistics can be provided for a particular scope or at the server level, the latter of which shows the aggregate of all scopes managed by that server.

ACTIVITY

Activity

1. Return to the DHCP console on the STUDENT1 server.

2. To view the DHCP address pool, expand **Superscope 110superscope**, expand **Scope[192.168.1.0] Team01**, and then click **Address Pool**. Locate the IP address range 192.168.1.1 - 192.168.1.200 (the IP address range allocated in Lab 4.3), and then locate the IP address range 192.168.1.1 - 192.168.1.2 (the IP address exclusions for the servers allocated in Lab 4.3).

3. To view the DHCP lease information, click **Address Leases**, and then review the lease information for the STUDENT1 server.

4. To view the DHCP reservations, click **Reservations**, and then review the reservations in the right pane.

5. To view the scope options, click **Scope Options**, and then review the scope options in the right pane.

6. To set the update interval and view DHCP server statistics, click **student1.domain1.classroom.com [192.168.1.1]**, click **Action** on the menu bar, click **Properties**, click the **General** tab, click the **Automatically update statistics every** check box, type **1** in the Minutes box, click **Apply**, click **OK**, right-click **student1.domain1.classroom.com [192.168.1.1]** in the console tree, and then click **Display Statistics**. Read the DHCP server statistics, and then click **Close** to close the DHCP statistics window.

7. Remain logged on to the STUDENT1 server for the next lab with the DHCP console open.

Certification Objectives

Objectives for Microsoft Exam #70-291: Implementing, Managing, and Maintaining a Microsoft Windows Server 2003 Network Infrastructure:

■ Manage DHCP

■ Troubleshoot DHCP

REVIEW QUESTIONS

1. You need to determine the expiration for a given computer on your Windows 2003 network. Which console line will you select?

   a. Address Pool

   b. Address Leases

   c. Reservations

   d. Scope Options

2. You need to determine which IP address for a given computer on your Windows 2003 network was matched to a physical address. Which console line will you select?

   a. Address Pool

   b. Address Leases

   c. Reservations

   d. Scope Options

   Using the following information provided from the DHCP server statistics, answer Questions 3 through 5:

   ```
   Start Time      1/6/2002 3:48:54 PM
   Up Time         379 Hours, 37 Minutes, 1 Second
   Discovers       14
   Offers          14
   Requests        1831
   Acks            15359
   Nacks           0
   Declines        0
   Releases        4
   Total Scopes    1
   In Use          11  (11%)
   Available       87  (88%)
   ```

3. How many DHCP client requests including renewals have occurred for an IP address?

   a. 14

   b. 1831

   c. 15359

   d. 4

4. How many DHCP server initial responses have there been to a client for an IP address?

a. 14

b. 1831

c. 15359

d. 4

5. How many additional computers might be able to receive an IP address?

a. 4

b. 14

c. 11

d. 87

LAB 5.3 DHCP AUDIT LOGGING

Objectives

The goal of this lab is to use DHCP audit logging to maintain the health of the DHCP service.

Materials Required

This lab will require the following:

- STUDENT1 server access

- Completion of Labs 5.1 through 5.2

Estimated completion time: **15 minutes**

Activity Background

From the DHCP audit log, you can determine when the DHCP service was started and stopped. In addition, information is available for all DHCP client actions involving the DHCP server.

ACTIVITY

Activity

1. Return to the DHCP console on the STUDENT1 computer.

2. To initiate audit logging, click **student1.domain1.classroom.com [192.168.1.1]** click **Action** on the menu bar, click **Properties**, click the **General** tab, verify the **Enable DHCP audit logging** is checked, and then click **OK**.

3. To open the DHCP log, click **Start**, click **Notepad**, click **File** on the menu bar, click **Open**, click the **Look in** drop-down arrow, click **Local Disk (C:)**, double-click **WINDOWS**, double-click the **system32**, double-click **dhcp**, click the Files of type drop-down arrow, click **All Files**, click **DhcpSrvLog-XXX.log** (where *XXX* is the code for a day of the week), and then click **Open**.

4. Review the DHCP log and then close Notepad.

5. Remain logged on for the next lab with the DHCP console open.

Certification Objectives

Objectives for Microsoft Exam #70-291: Implementing, Managing, and Maintaining a Microsoft Windows Server 2003 Network Infrastructure:

- Manage DHCP

- Troubleshoot DHCP

REVIEW QUESTIONS

1. You are wondering why you have to work on the Fourth of July. To make matters worse, it is a Monday. You are searching for the DHCP log file that was generated Friday. What file will you be looking for, and where is it located?

    a. \winnt\system32\dhcp\DhcpSrvLog.Fri

    b. \WINDOWS\system32\dhcp\DhcpSrvLog.Fri

    c. \winnt\system32\dhcp\DhcpSrvLog-Fri.log

    d. \WINDOWS\system32\dhcp\DhcpSrvLog-Fri.log

5

2. Your study group meets in 45 minutes. You have to pick a discussion topic for the next meeting, so you choose the DHCP log. You want to be helpful so you create a brief list of the items that are in the DHCP server log. Which of the following would most likely appear in a DHCP log? (Choose all that apply.)

a. A list of the relevant event codes with a description of each

b. Date and time a client was leased an IP address

c. The IP address and MAC address of a client

d. THE DATE AND TIME A CLIENT LEASE EXPIRED

Use the following segment from a DHCP log to answer Questions 3 through 5.

```
ID,Date,Time,Description,IP Address,Host Name,MAC Address
24,09/27/04,00:00:50,Database Cleanup Begin,,,,
25,09/27/04,00:00:50,0 leases expired and 0 leases
deleted,,,,
11,09/27/04,00:14:47,Renew,192.168.10.2,student2.,
00B0D05286F0,
12,09/27/04,12:51:10,Release,192.168.10.2,student2.,
00B0D05286F0,
01,09/27/04,14:56:48,Stopped,,,,
00,09/27/04,14:56:57,Started,,,,
55,09/27/04,14:56:58,Authorized(servicing),,classroom.com,
```

3. When did the DHCP server start the cleanup of the DHCP database?

a. On September 27, 2004 at 00:00:50

b. On September 27, 2004 at 00:14:47

c. On September 27, 2004 at 12:51:10

d. On September 27, 2004 at 14:56:48

e. On September 27, 2004 at 14:56:58

4. When was the DHCP server checked against the list of servers in Active Directory?

a. On September 27, 2004 at 00:00:50

b. On September 27, 2004 at 00:14:47

c. On September 27, 2004 at 12:51:10

d. On September 27, 2004 at 14:56:48

e. On September 27, 2004 at 14:56:58

5. What record indicates that the STUDENT2 server renewed its lease?

    a. 11,09/27/04,00:14:47,Renew,192.168.10.2,student2.,00B0D05286F0,

    b. 12,09/27/04,12:51:10,Release,192.168.10.2,student2.,00B0D05286F0,

    c. 01,09/27/04,14:56:48,Stopped,,,,

    d. 00,09/27/04,14:56:57,Started,,,,

    e. 55,09/27/04,14:56:58,Authorized(servicing),,classroom.com,,

5

LAB 5.4 USING CONFLICT DETECTION

Objectives

The goal of this lab is to minimize duplicate IP addresses on the network.

Materials Required

This lab will require the following:

- STUDENT1 server access

- Completion of Labs 5.1 through 5.3

Estimated completion time: **10 minutes**

Activity Background

The DHCP server uses the ICMP Echo Request/Reply (ping) process to test available scope IP addresses before including these addresses in DHCP lease offers to clients.

ACTIVITY

Activity

1. Return to the DHCP console on the STUDENT1 computer.

2. To initiate conflict detection, click **student1.domain1.classroom.com [192.168.1.1]**, click **Action** on the menu bar, click **Properties**, click the **Advanced** tab, type **2** in the Conflict detection attempts text box, click **Apply**, and then click **OK**.

3. Remain logged on for the next lab with the DHCP console open.

Certification Objectives

Objectives for Microsoft Exam #70-291: Implementing, Managing, and Maintaining a Microsoft Windows Server 2003 Network Infrastructure:

■ Manage DHCP

■ Troubleshoot DHCP

REVIEW QUESTIONS

1. You work as a network administrator for Colossal Trucks, the truck store that sells very large trucks. Your boss has been reading about conflict detection for Windows Server 2003 networks. He is advocating for your site to use conflict detection. You are concerned about the performance hit on your DHCP server when conflict detection is used. You check your inventory and you have no client computers running operating systems prior to Windows 2000. Which of the following will you discuss with your boss? (Choose all that apply.)

   a. Legacy systems that can be configured to use gratuitous ARPs

   b. Windows 2000 and later systems that use gratuitous ARPs

   c. Legacy systems that require conflict resolution

   d. Windows 2000 and later systems that require conflict resolution

2. You share the network administration role with Bob. Bob remarked that he has been tweaking the DHCP server. You get a call from the Helpdesk at your firm. They are concerned that the DHCP server is running slower than usual. You suspect that Bob changed the lease time, but when you check, the lease value is the same. What other configuration parameters might you consider checking?

   a. Conflict detection attempts set above 2

   b. Gratuitous ARPS

   c. Conflict resolution

   d. Conflict detection attempts set below 2

3. You are proud of the fact that you are very knowledgeable with the various TCP/IP protocols. Which TCP/IP protocols are used to perform conflict detection on a Windows Server 2003 DHCP server? (Choose all that apply.)

    a. IGMP echo request

    b. IGMP echo reply

    c. ICMP echo request

    d. ICMP echo reply

    e. ICMP ping request

    f. ICMP ping reply

Lab 5.5 Viewing DHCP Events in Event Viewer

Objectives

The goal of this lab is to use Event Viewer to view the System log for potential DHCP server problems.

Materials Required

This lab will require the following:

- STUDENT1 server access

- Completion of Labs 5.1 through 5.4

Estimated completion time: **15 minutes**

Activity Background

Event Viewer maintains logs about system events on your computer.

You will want to define your event log size and log wrapping (to overwrite as needed, clear manually, or overwrite after a specified number of days) to match your network requirements.

ACTIVITY

Activity

1. Remain at the STUDENT1 computer.

2. To open Event Viewer, click **Start**, point to **Administrative Tools**, and then click **Event Viewer**.

3. To select the system log, click **System**.

4. To create a filter for DHCP events, click **View** on the menu bar, click **Filter**, click the **Event source** drop-down arrow, scroll down the list and click **DHCPServer**, click **Apply**, and then click **OK**.

5. To view the details of an entry, double-click the selected entry. After reviewing the entry details, click **Cancel**.

 Use the up and down arrows on the upper-right corner to access additional event entries.

6. To view the properties dialog box for the system log, right-click **System**, and then click **Properties**.

7. To clear and save the system log, click **Clear Log**, click **Yes** to save the System log, type **SystemSave***MMDDYYYY* (where *MMDDYYYY* is today's date), and then click **Save**.

8. To set the maximum log size, type **24000** (or a value greater than the current value) in the Maximum log size box, and then click **Apply**.

9. To specify the action to overwrite the log when the log fills up, click the **Overwrite events older than** option button, review the number of days in the days text box, and then click **Apply**.

 If you want to archive the log at regular intervals, click the Overwrite events older than option button, and then specify the appropriate number of days, being sure that the maximum log size is large enough to accommodate the selected interval.

10. To restore the default settings, click **Restore Defaults**, click **Yes**, and then click **OK** twice.

11. Close Event Viewer and the DHCP computer, but remain logged on to the STUDENT1 server.

Certification Objectives

Objectives for Microsoft Exam #70-291: Implementing, Managing, and Maintaining a Microsoft Windows Server 2003 Network Infrastructure:

- Manage DHCP

- Troubleshoot DHCP

REVIEW QUESTIONS

1. You install Windows Server 2003 on a computer. TCP/IP is the only networking protocol installed on the computer. The computer is configured as a DHCP client. When you restart the computer, you receive the message "One or more services failed to start." Where do you go to find additional information about the failed services?

   a. Device manager

   b. Event viewer

   c. DHCP console

   d. Command prompt

2. Which is the easiest way to view only the DHCP entries on the system log?

   a. Select the DHCP entries with Export list.

   b. Choose columns and enter DHCP for the column selection.

   c. Click on the source button.

   d. Select the entries with the filter dialog.

3. How would you save a copy of the system log?

   a. Run System /save from a command prompt.

   b. Open Event viewer and click on the Save Log File As button.

   c. Open Event viewer and click on the Clear Log button.

   d. Open Event viewer and click on the System Log Backup button.

4. You and Bob share the role of network administrators for your network. Bob calls you over to a Windows Server 2003 computer. You see that he has Event Viewer open. He has changed the event log settings for the system log. The settings he picked don't look right. You would like to reset them to more reasonable values. What would be the easiest way to reset the system log settings?

   a. Run System /reset from a command prompt.

   b. Open Event viewer and click the Reset button.

   c. Open Event viewer and click the Restore Defaults button.

   d. Open Event viewer and click the System Log Backup button.

5

LAB 5.6 TROUBLESHOOTING DHCP

Objectives

The goal of this lab is to identify and resolve problems related to the DHCP service.

Materials Required

The lab will require the following:

- STUDENT2 server access

- Completion of Labs 5.1 through 5.5

Estimated completion time: **15 minutes**

Activity Background

As a network administrator you are responsible for the well-being of your network. You must be prepared to troubleshoot a key component of your network—the DHCP service.

Activity

1. Go to the STUDENT2 server. Logon to the STUDENT2 computer as **Administrator** with the password **secret**.

2. To display the Internet Protocol (TCP/IP) Properties dialog box, click **Start**, point to **Control Panel**, point to **Network Connections**, click **Local Area Connection**, click **Properties**, click **Internet Protocol (TCP/IP)**, and then click **Properties**.

3. To practice setting up an alternate configuration, click the **General** tab, click the **Obtain an IP address automatically** check box to select it, click the **Alternate Configuration** tab, click **User configured**, type **192.168.0.250** in the IP address text box, verify the Subnet mask is **255.255.255.0**, type **192.168.0.1** in the Default gateway text box, type **24.218.131.1** in the Preferred DNS server text box, review your settings, click **Cancel** twice, and then click **Close**.

Incorrectly editing the registry may severely damage your system. Before making changes to the registry, you should back up any valued data on the computer.

4. To open the Registry Editor, click **Start**, click **Run**, type **regedt32** in the Open text box (there is no I in regedt32), and then click the **OK** button.

5. To navigate to the Parameters subfield in the registry to modify, expand **HKEY_LOCAL_MACHINE**, expand **SYSTEM**, expand **CurrentControlSet**, expand **Services**, scroll and expand **Tcpip**, and then expand **Parameters**.

6. To back up the Parameters subkey, click the **Parameters** folder, click the **File** menu, click **Export**, type **regback** in the File name text box, and then click the **Save** button.

7. To disable APIPA, click **Parameters**, click **Edit** on the menu bar, click **New**, click **DWORD Value**, type **IPAutoconfigurationEnabled** to replace the default text, press **Enter**, right-click **IPAutoconfigurationEnabled**, click **Modify**, verify that the Edit DWORD Value setting is **0**, and then click **Cancel**.

8. Close the Registry Editor, close any open windows, and shutdown the STUDENT2 server.

9. Go to the STUDENT1 server, close any open windows, and then shutdown the server.

Certification Objectives

Objectives for Microsoft Exam #70-291: Implementing, Managing, and Maintaining a Microsoft Windows Server 2003 Network Infrastructure:

■ Troubleshoot DHCP

REVIEW QUESTIONS

1. You install Windows Server 2003 on your new computer. You configure the computer to request an IP address and configuration from the DHCP server. Next, you open a command prompt window and type ipconfig /all. You view the following on the screen:

```
c:\>ipconfig /all
Windows IP Configuration
        Host Name . . . . . . . . . . . . : student2
        Primary DNS Suffix  . . . . . . . :
        Node Type . . . . . . . . . . . . : Hybrid
        IP Routing Enabled. . . . . . . . : No
        WINS Proxy Enabled. . . . . . . . : No
Ethernet adapter Local Area Connection:
        Connection-specific DNS Suffix  . :
        Description . . . . . . . . . . . : 3Com 3C920
                                            Integrated Fast
                                            Ethernet Controller
                                            (3C905C-TX Compatible
        Physical Address. . . . . . . . . : 00-B0-D0-52-8D-1C
        DHCP Enabled. . . . . . . . . . . : Yes
        Autoconfiguration Enabled . . . . : Yes
        Autoconfiguration IP Address. . . : 169.254.177.247
        Subnet Mask . . . . . . . . . . . : 255.255.0.0
        Default Gateway . . . . . . . . . :
        DNS Servers . . . . . . . . . . . :
        Primary WINS Server . . . . . . . :
```

You focus on the IP address, and it is not the 192.168.1.0 network address that you expected. Which of the following are relevant to the problem at hand?

a. You need to run the regedt32 program to correct the problem.

b. You can resolve the problem by restarting the computer.

c. The DHCP server was not available when the DHCP request was made.

d. You have been assigned an IP address as a result of APIPA.

e. You need to configure the TCP/IP protocol to request a configuration from the DHCP server.

2. Juan works as a network administrator for a company that has a central office and four branch offices. The central office is on the 172.16.0.0 network. The branch offices are on the 172.21.0.0, 172.22.0.0, 172.23.0.0 and 172.24.0.0 networks. On the 172.16.0.0 network there is an IIS server that runs the company's intranet and an SNA server that connects to a mainframe. On each subnet there is a file and print server.

Juan works late the previous night and so sleeps in late the next morning. When he arrives, he finds that some users are having connectivity problems.

Two users at one branch office can't ping their local file server. In addition, they cannot ping any other servers in the company, but they can ping each other. These two users have the following IP addresses:

169.254.0.245

169.254.0.246

At another branch, there are five users that can ping each other but cannot ping their local file server. These four users have the following IP addresses:

169.254.1.60

169.254.1.91

169.254.1.102

169.254.1.103

What is the major issue, and what will Juan do to correct the problem?

a. Make sure that a DNS Server is available for all of the clients on the segment. Windows Server 2003 clients rely heavily on DNS resolution.

b. Some computers may have received APIPA addresses. Check to see if a functioning DHCP relay agent is available for their segment.

c. The computers are probably configured with static IP addresses. Change the computers over to obtain an address automatically.

d. The switch that the computers are connected to has broken. Replace the switch, and patch each system to the new switch.

3. You are the network administrator for a nonprofit organization that has deployed Windows Server 2003. Since you are using the 80/20 rule, you place scopes on the two DHCP servers. Within a few hours after authorizing the second DHCP server, you discover that some client computers have error messages indicating that duplicate IP addresses exit on your network.

You open the first DHCP server and review the scopes. You see the following on the DHCP console:

192.168.0.1	192.168.0.254	Address range for distribution
192.168.0.1	192.168.0.9	IP addresses excluded for distribution
192.168.0.201	192.168.0.254	IP addresses excluded for distribution
192.168.1.1	192.168.1.254	Address range for distribution
192.168.1.10	192.168.1.200	IP addresses excluded for distribution

You rush to the second server and open the DHCP console. You see the following scope information on the new server:

192.168.1.1	192.168.1.254	Address range for distribution
192.168.1.1	192.168.1.9	IP addresses excluded for distribution
192.168.1.201	192.168.1.254	IP addresses excluded for distribution
192.168.0.1	192.168.0.254	Address range for distribution
192.168.0.10	192.168.0.200	IP addresses excluded for distribution

What must you do to correct the problem?

a. From each server, turn on DHCP relication so that the scopes can be updated between the two servers.

b. From each server, reauthorize the servers so that the scopes can be reconciled between the two servers.

c. Correct the IP address exclusions for the 20% address exclusions on each DHCP server.

d. There should not be a problem, because the servers and routers are using static IP addresses.

4. Professor Boswell lectured on DHCP server last night. Instead of going home, one of Professor Boswell's students rushes straight to work. He has decided to jump in head first and do away with those static IP addresses. He configures his entire network for DHCP by installing a DHCP server on one of his subnets. He authorizes the server as Professor Boswell stressed. He picks a test computer on each subnet and sets up each test computer to obtain an IP address automatically. And this is really perplexing; it only works for clients that are on the same subnet as the DHCP server. The next day in class he discusses his problem with Professor Boswell. Professor Boswell smiles at Bob. What will he tell Bob to do to resolve his problem?

   a. Actually, he does not stop smiling and asks Bob to study more.

   b. He tells Bob to configure the DHCP Relay Agent service on one system in every subnet except the one where the DHCP server is located.

   c. He tells Bob to configure the DHCP Relay Agent service on the DHCP server.

   d. He tells Bob to configure the DHCP Relay Agent service on the subnet where the DHCP server is located.

5

5. You are the network administrator for a small branch office. The home office has assigned the IP network 192.168.160.0 for your use. You want to configure three ranges of addresses to be assigned by a DHCP server to computers on a specific subnet. The ranges are:

192.168.160.10 – 192.168.160.50

192.168.160.75 – 192.168.160.150

192.168.160.200 – 192.168.160.250

These are the only addresses that you want the DHCP server to assign. You use the default subnet mask 255.255.255.0. Which scope items will provide the correct DHCP configuration?

a. Scope 192.168.160.10 – 192.168.160.50

   Scope 192.168.160.75 – 192.168.160.150

   Scope 192.168.160.200– 192.168.160.250

b. Scope 192.168.160.1 – 192.168.160.254

   Exclusion 192.168.160.51 – 192.168.160.74

   Exclusion 192.168.160.151 – 192.168.160.199

c. Scope 192.168.160.10 – 192.168.160.250

   Exclusion 192.168.160.51 – 192.168.160.74

   Exclusion 192.168.160.151 – 192.168.160.199

d. Scope 192.168.160.10 – 192.168.160.250

   Static 192.168.160.51 – 192.168.160.74

   Static 192.168.160.151 – 192.168.160.199

6

CONFIGURING NAME RESOLUTION

Labs included in this chapter:

♦ Lab 6.1 Configuring Host and NetBIOS Names

♦ Lab 6.2 Configuring Host Name Resolution

♦ Lab 6.3 Configuring NetBIOS Name Resolution

Microsoft MCSE Exam #70-291 Objectives	
Objective	Lab
Install and Configure DNS Server Service	6.1, 6.2
Install and Configure WINS Service	6.1, 6.3

Name resolution is a client/server application. This chapter presents the client side of name resolution. In subsequent chapters, the server side of name resolution is covered: Chapter 7—Implementing and Managing the DNS Service and Chapter 8—Implementing and Managing WINS.

LAB 6.1 CONFIGURING HOST AND NETBIOS NAMES

Objectives

The goal of this lab is configure the two names that can be assigned to identify computers. Computers are assigned NetBIOS (Network Basic Input/Output System) names and host names.

Materials Required

This lab will require the following:

- STUDENT2 server access

- Completion of Labs 4.1 through 4.5

Estimated completion time: **30 minutes**

Activity Background

When you installed Windows Server 2003, you were asked to specify the computer name. The name you entered had to conform to the naming rules that your networking group uses.

Microsoft recommends that you use only Internet-standard characters in the computer name. The standard characters are the numbers 0 to 9, uppercase and lowercase letters from A to Z, and the hyphen (-) character. In addition, the recommended length of a computer name is 15 characters or less. Although you can assign a maximum length for a computer name of up to 63 characters, older operating systems recognize a computer by only the first 15 bytes of the name.

The host name is the name of a node on the IP network. The default host name is the computer name specified during installation.

A fully qualified domain name (FQDN) is the name that uniquely defines a server on the IP network, such as the Internet. An FQDN consists of a host, domain name, and a top-level domain, including the dot (.) for the root domain. For example, www.course.com. is a fully qualified domain name: www is the host, .course is the second-level domain, .com is the top level domain, and the dot at the end is for the root domain.

An FQDN always starts with a host name and continues all the way up to the top-level domain name, so www.networking.course.com is also an FQDN. See Figure 6-1 for the network hierarchy for www.networking.course.com. In this illustration, the organization "course" created a subdomain called networking. A subdomain is a domain that is part of a larger domain name. Network administrators create subdomains to divide the domain namespace for ease of administration.

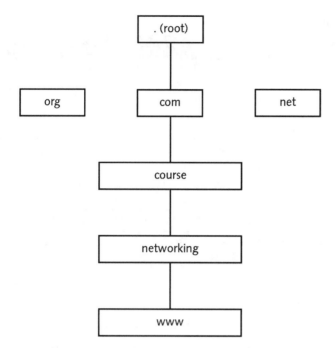

Figure 6-1   FQDN for www.networking.course.com

During name resolution, FQDN names are searched from right to left on the Internet. For the FQDN, www.networking.course.com in Figure 6-1, the search would start with the root (the dot), proceed to the .com top-level domain, continue with the .course domain, the .networking subdomain, and finish with the host www. The DNS (Domain Name System) resolves FQDN to IP addresses.

The NetBIOS is an application programming interface (API), which is used by programmers to access services on a LAN. Examples of these services are name management and session management. In addition, NetBIOS provides services to send datagrams between nodes on a LAN.

NetBIOS names are always 15 characters in length. Recall that the computer name is 15 characters and that you can specify these characters. For NetBIOS names, the 16th character of the NetBIOS name (expressed as a hexadecimal number 00–FF) always indicates a resource type. The NetBIOS name space is flat—meaning that names can be used only once within a network.

NetBIOS names are dynamically registered on the network when computers start up, services start, or users log on. NetBIOS names can be registered as unique or as group names. Unique names have one address mapped with a name. Group names have more than one address tied to a name. Table 6-1 provides a list of resources that you might encounter as a network administrator.

Table 6-1   NetBIOS name types

Format	Type	Description
Computer_name [00h]	Unique	Registered by the Workstation service (NetBIOS computer name)
Computer_name [03h]	Unique	Messenger service to send/receive messages
User_name [03h]	Unique	Currently logged on user
Computer_name [20h]	Unique	Registered by the Server service to provide file sharing on the network
Domain_name [00h]	Group	Registered by the Workstation Service to receive browser requests
Group_name [1Eh]	Group	Normal group name (broadcast to group)
__MSBROWSE__ [01h]	Group	Registered by master browser (tracks computers sharing resources)

ACTIVITY

Activity

1. Log on to the STUDENT2 server as **Administrator** with a password of **secret**.

2. To verify the host name, click **Start**, right-click **My Computer**, click **Properties**, click the **Computer Name** tab, and then verify that the full computer name is **STUDENT2**.

3. To add a description for the STUDENT2 server, click in the Computer description text box, type **Lab Server – STUDENT2**, and then click **Apply**.

To verify the NetBIOS name, click **Change**, click **More**, verify that the NetBIOS computer name is **STUDENT2**, and then click **Cancel** three times.

NOTE

4. Remain on the STUDENT2 server for the next lab.

Certification Objectives

Objectives for Microsoft Exam #70-291: Implementing, Managing, and Maintaining a Microsoft Windows Server 2003 Network Infrastructure:

- Install and Configure DNS Server Service

- Install and Configure WINS

REVIEW QUESTIONS

1. You are preparing a handout for the next study group meeting. Professor Boswell has lectured on computer names. You create a list of possible computer names. You ask Helga to review the list and indicate which names are invalid. Which names will Helga indicate are not valid computer names based on the Microsoft recommendations? (Choose all that apply.)

   a. student2

   b. Host-1

   c. Thisisaverylongcomputername

   d. HIT@#$%

   e. HOST#1

   f. hOsToFcApS

   g. 123computer

2. You continue with your preparation for the presentation for the next study group meeting. You want to include a section on NetBIOS names. Which of the following will you include as valid characteristics of NetBIOS? (Choose all that apply.)

   a. NetBIOS is used by programmers to access LAN services.

   b. NetBIOS can send datagrams between computers.

   c. NetBios names can be up to 63 characters in length.

   d. Computers register their NetBIOS names when Office applications start.

   e. Group names are restricted to single computers.

3. Which name resolution protocol is the most commonly used in large environments, including the Internet?

   a. hosts

   b. lmhosts

   c. WINS

   d. DNS

   e. arp

4. A NetBIOS name is a unique address of how many characters (bytes)?

   a. 8

   b. 16

   c. 24

   d. 32

   e. 63

5. What is the order in which a server named spurs.basketball.sports.com would be located in a typical DNS request?

   a. Root --> sports servers --> Characters

   b. Root --> COM servers --> Characters --> spurs server

   c. Root --> COM servers --> sports servers --> basketball servers --> spurs server

   d. spurs server --> basketball server --> sports server --> com servers

   e. spurs.basketball server --> sports server --> com servers

---

LAB 6.2 CONFIGURING HOST NAME RESOLUTION

Objectives

The goal of this lab is configure host name resolution. In addition, host name resolution will be explored. The host name is the name of a node on an IP network. In order to send packets to a node by name, the host name must be resolved (or translated) from a host name to an IP address. This resolution is accomplished by the DNS resolver, which executes on the client computer.

Materials Required

This lab will require the following:

- STUDENT2 server access

- Completion of Lab 6.1

Estimated completion time: **15 minutes**

Activity Background

Why is the DNS client called a resolver? The DNS resolver facilitates the resolution of host names for the TCP/IP applications executed on the client computer.

The host name must be the same as the current computer, a name in the hosts file, or it must be known by a DNS server for that host to be found when attempting to communicate with it. The hosts file maps host names to IP addresses. The DNS server provides IP addresses for the host names in the DNS zone files.

The hosts file is a simple text file that contains the necessary fields to provide host name resolution. To resolve a host name, the resolver reads the hosts file one line at a time to locate a host name. The user of each computer is required to update the hosts file with additions, deletions, and changes. An alternative to manual updates would be to copy the hosts file from a central server.

Each line of the hosts file contains a number of fields that appear in this order:

- A single IP address followed by at least one space

- One or more corresponding FQDN(s)

- One or more host names (optional)

- A comment preceded by a pound sign (#) (optional)

Hosts files only work when there are a limited number of hosts to resolve. DNS servers, with a distributed database of host names, are used to provide name resolution for larger networks. Each DNS server is responsible for maintaining a database of host names for its local area of the network.

To provide faster host name resolution, the DNS resolver places entries in a DNS resolver cache on the local computer. At system startup (or when the hosts file is updated), the hosts file is loaded into the DNS cache. For a period of time, defined as the Time to Live (TTL), any names previously resolved by DNS are added to the DNS resolver cache. The DNS resolver supports negative caching of unresolved or nonvalid DNS names. These entries are added by the DNS resolver in response to a negative answer from a DNS server for a queried name. The DNS resolver places an entry for the host with a message which indicates that no records matched the DNS query.

Activity

1. Verify that you are logged onto the STUDENT2 server.

2. To open the Command Prompt window, click **Start**, and then click **Command Prompt**.

3. To determine the host name for a computer, type **hostname** at the command prompt, and press **Enter**. Your output should resemble the following:

```
C:\Documents and Settings\Administrator>hostname
STUDENT2
```

4. To clear the DNS resolver cache, type **ipconfig /flushdns** at the command prompt, and then press **Enter**. Your output should resemble the following:

```
C:\Documents and Settings\Administrator>ipconfig /flushdns
Windows IP Configuration
Successfully flushed the DNS Resolver Cache.
```

5. To open the hosts file in Notepad, click **Start**, point to **All Programs**, point to **Accessories**, click **Notepad**, click **File** on the menu bar, click **Open**, click the **Files of type** drop-down arrow, click **All Files**, click the **Look in** drop-down arrow, click **Local Disk (C:)**, double-click **WINDOWS**, scroll and double-click **system32**, double-click **drivers**, double-click **etc**, click the **hosts** file, and then click **Open**.

6. To add a host entry into the hosts file (for a computer that does not exist today), click on the blank line after 127.0.0.1 localhost, type **192.168.1.249 phantom**, click **File** on the menu bar, click **Save**, and then close **Notepad**.

7. Return to the Command Prompt window, type **ping phantom**, and then press **Enter**. Your output should resemble the following. (The "Request timed out" appears because the phantom only exists in the movies.)

```
C:\Documents and Settings\Administrator>ping phantom
Pinging phantom [192.168.10.249 with 32 bytes of data:
Request timed out.
Request timed out.
Request timed out.
Request timed out.
```

8. To display the phantom's entry in the DNS resolver cache, type **ipconfig / displaydns**, and then press **Enter**. Scroll and locate the output that should resemble the following:

```
phantom
----------------------------------------
Record Name . . . . . : phantom
Record Type . . . . . : 1
Time To Live  . . . . : 596923
Data Length . . . . . : 4
Section . . . . . . . : Answer
A (Host) Record . . . : 192.168.1.249
```

9. To verify the IP address of the DNS server, type **ipconfig /all**, and then press **Enter**. Scroll and locate the DNS server's entry of 192.168.1.1 in output that should resemble the following:

```
C:\Documents and Settings\Administrator>ipconfig /all

Windows IP Configuration

        Host Name . . . . . . . . . . . . : student2
        Primary Dns Suffix  . . . . . . . :
        Node Type . . . . . . . . . . . . : Hybrid
        IP Routing Enabled. . . . . . . . : Yes
        WINS Proxy Enabled. . . . . . . . : No

Ethernet adapter Local Area Connection:

        Connection-specific DNS Suffix  . :
        Description . . . . . . . . . . . : 3Com 3C920 Integrated
                                            Fast Ethernet
                                            Controller
                                            (3C905C-TX
                                            Compatible)
        Physical Address. . . . . . . . . : 00-B0-D0-52-86-F0
        DHCP Enabled. . . . . . . . . . . : No
        IP Address. . . . . . . . . . . . : 192.168.1.2
        Subnet Mask . . . . . . . . . . . : 255.255.255.0
        Default Gateway . . . . . . . . . :
        DHCP Class ID . . . . . . . . . . :
        DNS Servers . . . . . . . . . . . : 192.168.1.1
```

10. To verify the DNS advanced configuration, click **Start**, point to **Control Panel**, point to **Network Connections**, click **Local Area Connection**, click **Properties**, click **Internet Protocol (TCP/IP)**, click **Properties**, click **Advanced**, click the **DNS** tab, review the **DNS server addresses, in order of use** list, verify that the **Append primary and connection specific DNS suffixes** option button is selected, verify that the **Append parent suffixes of the primary DNS suffix** check box is checked, verify that the **Register this connection's addresses in DNS** check box is checked, click **Cancel** three times, and then click **Close**.

11. Remain on the STUDENT2 server for the next lab with the command prompt window open.

Certification Objectives

Objectives for Microsoft Exam #70-291: Implementing, Managing, and Maintaining a Microsoft Windows Server 2003 Network Infrastructure:

- Install and Configure DNS Server Service

REVIEW QUESTIONS

1. What utility provides a view of the contents of the DNS resolver cache?

   a. nbtstat

   b. ipconfig

   c. hostname

   d. netlister

   e. ping

2. You manage 200 computers running Windows 2000 Professional and Windows XP. One of the computers is resolving the name of a server incorrectly. Which of the following is the correct command to clear the DNS resolver cache?

   a. ipconfig /clearresolvercache

   b. ipconfig /flushresolvercache

   c. ipconfig /cleardns

   d. ipconfig /flushdns

   e. ipconfig /collapsedns

3. You are practicing how to use the ipconfig command-line utility in the server lab after class. You use the ipconfig command to display the contents of the DNS Resolver cache. You see an entry on the screen with the message "Negative cache entry for no records." You ask Bob for an explanation. What reason will Bob give you for the error message?

   a. The resolver needs to clear the resolver cache.

   b. The resolver placed a static entry in the cache to eliminate "no records."

   c. The resolver attempted to dynamically update a host, and the record was rejected by the master DNS.

   d. The resolver made a query to DNS, and the host name could not be resolved.

4. While configuring the advanced TCP/IP configuration parameters of your Windows Server 2003, you view the following TCP/IP properties as shown in Figure 6-2.

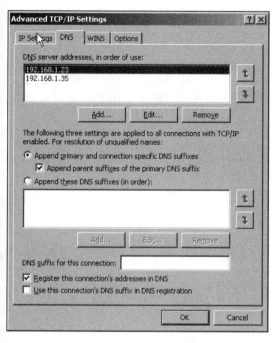

Figure 6-2 Advanced TCP/IP properties

Which of the following statements is true? (Choose all that apply.)

a. The alternate DNS is 192.168.1.35.

b. The primary DNS is 192.168.1.23.

c. The alternate DNS is 192.168.1.23.

d. This server will register its connection in DNS dynamically.

e. To reverse the order of the two IP addresses, press the down arrow.

5. You are the network administrator at a "top secret" shop. You want to place a reference on a single Windows Server 2003 to enable the resolution of another computer. How will you accomplish this task without compromising the integrity of your network?

a. Place a static entry in the resolver cache.

b. Force a secure entry in the resolver cache.

c. Add an entry to the hosts file.

d. Place an entry in the resolver file.

Lab 6.3 Configuring NetBIOS Name Resolution

Objectives

The goal of this lab is to configure NetBIOS name resolution. In addition, NetBIOS name resolution will be explored. The NetBIOS name is the name of a computer on a NetBIOS network. In order to send packets to a computer by NetBIOS name, the NetBIOS name must be resolved (or translated) from a NetBIOS name to an IP address. This resolution is accomplished by the NetBIOS client that executes on the client computer.

Materials Required

This lab will require the following:

- STUDENT2 server access

- Completion of Labs 6.1 and 6.2

Estimated completion time: **15 minutes**

Activity Background

A NetBIOS name can be resolved to an IP address by four methods:

- The local NetBIOS name cache

- A Windows Internet Naming Server (WINS)

- Broadcasts (b-node)

- The local lmhosts file

Should these four methods fail, the hosts file and DNS could be used for the NetBIOS name to IP address resolution. The six steps for NetBIOS name resolution are presented in Figure 6-3.

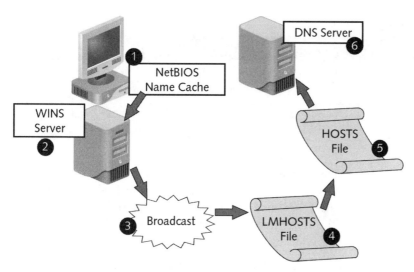

Figure 6-3   NetBIOS name resolution sequence

To remember the NetBIOS resolution sequence, use this learning aide: "Can We Buy Large Hard Drives?"

TIP

Windows operating systems set aside an area of memory that contains the recently resolved NetBIOS names and their corresponding IP addresses. Each entry in the NetBIOS name cache has a TTL assigned. This is the first place for NetBIOS name resolution.

Should the NetBIOS name not be found in the NetBIOS name cache, a WINS server, if configured, could be contacted. The WINS server checks its database for name. If the name is found, the WINS server returns the IP address to the client computer. The client computer adds the entry to the local name cache.

If the name is not found on the WINS server, the process goes to the next step. The client initiates a broadcast, a shout, to the network for the computer. All computers are interrupted with the broadcast. Should a computer have the requested NetBIOS name, it will respond with its IP address.

If no computer responds to the broadcast, the client checks its lmhosts file (assuming that it was configured to use the lmhosts file). The lmhosts file is similar to the hosts file and contains IP addresses and NetBIOS names. The entire lmhosts file is parsed including comments on each lookup. Table 6-2 lists tags that a network administrator might encounter in the lmhosts file.

Table 6-2 Tags in lmhosts file

Tag	Description
#	Comment or follows # character
#PRE	Load into the NetBIOS cache at startup
#DOM	Associate NetBIOS name with a NetBIOS domain
#INCLUDE <filename>	Seek the specified <filename> and parse it as if it were local

Should the first four steps not succeed, the process continues with the hosts file and the DNS server. The FQDN is constructed by appending the DNS suffix to the NetBIOS name. And what happens if these two last steps also fail? NetBIOS name resolution can not be used to determine the IP address of the other computer. The computer can only be contacted by using the IP address.

NetBIOS names are registered with WINS. Registration occurs when the computer starts, a user logs on, or a NetBIOS service starts. For example, when the Server service starts, this service registers a unique NetBIOS name. The exact name registered is a combination of the characters assigned for the NetBIOS computer name plus a 16th hexadecimal character. If the computer name is STUDENT2, and the Server service starts, the registered name will be STUDENT2 20. The 20 represents the hexadecimal byte value of "20" or [20h] as it appears when viewing NETBIOS name registrations. The codes were previously presented in Table 6-1.

NetBIOS name resolution is required for "legacy" computers. Legacy operating systems are pre-Windows 2000 operating systems, such as Windows 9x and Windows NT.

ACTIVITY

Activity

1. Verify that you are logged onto the STUDENT2 server with the Command Prompt window open.

2. To open the lmhosts file in Notepad, click **Start**, click **Notepad**, click **File** on the menu bar, click **Open**, click the **Files of type** drop-down arrow, click **All Files**, click the **Look in** drop-down arrow, click **Local Disk (C:)**, double-click **WINDOWS**, scroll and double-click **system32**, double-click **drivers**, double-click **etc**, click **lmhosts.sam**, and then click **Open**.

3. View the contents of the lmhosts file. Scroll and locate the **The following example illustrates all of these extensions** text, and then review the sample entries.

4. To view the contents of the NetBIOS cache, type **nbtstat -c** at the command prompt, and then press **Enter**. Your output should resemble the following:

```
C:\Documents and Settings\Administrator>nbtstat -c
Local Area Connection:
Node IpAddress: [192.168.1.2] Scope Id: []

            NetBIOS Remote Cache Name Table

    Name              Type       Host Address      Life [sec]
    --------------------------------------------------------------
    STUDENT1      <20>  UNIQUE        192.168.1.1       315
    COURSE        <1B>  UNIQUE        192.168.1.1       315
```

NOTE

If your server has not previously resolved any NetBIOS names, your NetBIOS cache may be empty.

5. To view the registrations for the computer, type **nbtstat −n**, and then press **Enter**. Your output should resemble the following:

```
C:\Documents and Settings\Administrator>nbtstat −n

Local Area Connection:
Node IpAddress: [192.168.1.2] Scope Id: []

            NetBIOS Local Name Table

    Name              Type       Status
    -------------------------------------------------
    STUDENT2      <00>  UNIQUE     Registered
    WORKGROUP     <00>  GROUP      Registered
    STUDENT2      <20>  UNIQUE     Registered
    WORKGROUP     <1E>  GROUP      Registered
    WORKGROUP     <1D>  UNIQUE     Registered
    .._MSBROWSE_.<01>  GROUP      Registered
```

6. To release and refresh the registrations with WINS, type **nbtstat −RR**, and then press **Enter**. Your output should resemble the following:

```
C:\Documents and Settings\Administrator>nbtstat −RR
The NetBIOS names registered by this computer have
been refreshed.
```

7. To verify the WINS advanced configuration, click **Start**, point to **Control Panel**, point to **Network Connections**, click **Local Area Connection**, click **Properties**, click **Internet Protocol (TCP/IP)**, click **Properties**, click **Advanced**, click the **WINS** tab, note that there are no **WINS addresses**, verify that the **Enable LMHOSTS lookup** check box is selected, verify that the **Default: Use NetBIOS setting from the DHCP server. If static IP address is used or the DHCP server does not provide NetBIOS setting, enable NetBIOS over TCP/IP** option button is checked, click **Cancel** three times, and then click **Close**.

If you disable NetBIOS over TCP/IP, you may not be able to connect to computers that are running operating systems prior to Windows 2000.

CAUTION

8. Close any open windows and shutdown STUDENT2.

Certification Objectives

Objectives for Microsoft Exam #70-291: Implementing, Managing, and Maintaining a Microsoft Windows Server 2003 Network Infrastructure:

■ Install and Configure WINS

REVIEW QUESTIONS

1. You are about to create entries in a lmhosts file. Which of the following errors will cause an entry to be invalid and result in the lmhosts file being unable to resolve NetBIOS names to IP addresses? (Choose all that apply.)

   a. all uppercase letters in the NetBIOS name

   b. invalid IP address

   c. NetBIOS name listed first, then the IP address

   d. IP address listed first, then the NetBIOS name

   e. mixed upper- and lowercase letters in the NetBIOS name

2. Which of the following utilities provides a view of the contents of the NetBIOS cache?

   a. nbtstat

   b. ipconfig

   c. hostname

   d. netlister

   e. ping

3. You are the network administrator for a Windows Server 2003 network. Your network has a mixture of Windows clients, including Windows 95 and Windows NT. You have the following goals for your network design:

1 Resolving host names

2 Resolving NetBIOS names

Your solution is to configure DHCP scope with the IP addressees of both a DNS and a WINS server. Which goal is met?

a. Goal 1 is met

b. Goal 2 is met

c. Goals 1 and 2 are met

d. Neither goals are met

4. Which of the following methods is used to resolve NetBIOS names to IP addresses? (Choose all that apply.)

a. NetBIOS name cache

b. resolver name cache

c. WINS server

d. multicast

e. DNS server

f. hosts file

5. You are the network administrator for a Windows Server 2003 network. Your network has a mixture of Windows desktop boxes, including computers with "legacy" operating systems. You would like to eliminate the NetBIOS traffic on your network. After a review of NetBIOS over TCP/IP, you are considering turning off NetBIOS over TCP/IP in the DHCP scope for your network. What will the impact be of this decision regarding the "legacy" operating systems?

a. NetBIOS programs will not be able to operate over TCP/IP.

b. NetBIOS operations will be translated into DNS operations.

c. Windows 2003 servers will emulate the NetBIOS environment for the older operating systems.

d. The will be no problems with this decision.

7

IMPLEMENTING AND MANAGING THE DNS SERVICE

Labs included in this chapter:

- ◆ Lab 7.1 Installing the DNS Service
- ◆ Lab 7.2 Configuring the DNS Server Service
- ◆ Lab 7.3 Configuring DNS Zones
- ◆ Lab 7.4 Testing the DNS Server Service
- ◆ Lab 7.5 Managing Dynamic Update
- ◆ Lab 7.6 Monitoring DNS Performance

Microsoft MCSE Exam #70-291 Objectives	
Objective	Lab
Install and Configure the DNS Server Service	7.1, 7.2, 7.3, 7.4, 7.5
Manage DNS	7.2, 7.3, 7.4, 7.5
Monitor DNS	7.4, 7.6

Lab 7.1 Installing the DNS Service

Objective

The goal of this lab is to install the DNS (Domain Name System) Server Service.

Materials Required

This lab will require the following:

- STUDENT1 and STUDENT2 server access

- A Windows Server 2003 Installation CD-ROM

- Completion of Lab 4.1, which provides the Active Directory Integrated DNS that will be used as the primary, or master, DNS

Estimated completion time: **30 minutes**

Activity Background

DNS provides a system for naming computers and network services that is organized into a hierarchy of domains. DNS naming is used in TCP/IP networks to locate computers through user-friendly names. When a user types a DNS name in an application, DNS services can resolve the name to an IP address.

ACTIVITY

Activity

1. Logon to the STUDENT1 and STUDENT2 servers as **administrator** with the password **secret**.

2. Go to the STUDENT2 server.

3. Insert the Microsoft Windows Server 2003 CD-ROM. When the Microsoft Windows Server 2003 family window is displayed, click the **Exit** hyperlink.

4. To display the Internet Protocol (TCP/IP) dialog box for the STUDENT2 server, click **Start**, point to **Control Panel**, point to **Network Connections**, click **Local Area Connection**, click **Properties**, click **Internet Protocol (TCP/IP)**, and then click **Properties**.

5. To configure TCP/IP for the STUDENT2 server, click the **Use the following IP address** option button, type **192.168.1.2** in the IP address text box, press the **Tab** key, confirm that **255.255.255.0** appears in the Subnet mask text box, click in the Preferred DNS server text box, type **192.168.1.1**, click **OK**, and then click **Close** twice.

6. To open Add or Remove Programs, click **Start**, point to **Control Panel**, and then click **Add or Remove Programs**.

7. To install DNS, click the **Add/Remove Windows Components** icon, scroll and click **Networking Services** (the label and not the check box), click **Details**, click the **Domain Name System (DNS)** check box to select it, click **OK**, click **Next**, wait for the files to copy and the configuration to complete, and then click **Finish**.

8. Close the Add or Remove Programs window.

9. Remain logged on to the STUDENT2 server.

Certification Objectives

Objectives for Microsoft Exam #70-291: Implementing, Managing, and Maintaining a Microsoft Windows Server 2003 Network Infrastructure:

- Install and configure the DNS Server Service

7

REVIEW QUESTIONS

1. Betty is a network administrator and needs to install the DNS Server Service. What should she use to install the DNS service?

   a. Windows Server 2003 network service installer

   b. Add/Remove Programs

   c. Local Area Connection Properties

   d. The netinstall command from a Command Prompt window.

2. Ashley and Chrissy are discussing the various types of DNS servers. They have created a list of the characteristics of DNS servers. Help them match the characteristics with the descriptions of the following types of DNS servers:

Description	Characteristics
___ 1. Caching-only server	a. Caches answers from queries
___ 2. Primary server	b. Maintains zone records
___ 3. Secondary server	c. Offloads DNS query traffic
	d. Provides limited name resolution for primary server

3. The network at your company is set up as shown in Figure 7-1. Users at the Dallas and Houston offices are complaining about slow response times when they surf the Web. You monitor the network traffic over the network links from Austin to Dallas, and from Austin to Houston. You notice a number of repetitive host name resolutions over the two links. What can you do to correct the name resolution problem for the Dallas and Houston offices?

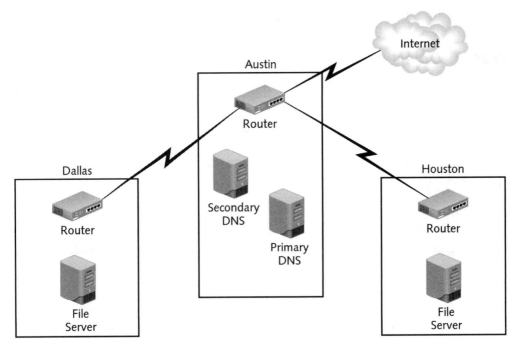

Figure 7-1   Your network

a. Purchase additional communication lines from Dallas and Houston to the Internet.

b. Place a Web resolution Helper on each of the remote routers.

c. Install a DNS caching server on the file servers at Dallas and Houston.

d. Install DNS host caching on the clients at Dallas and Houston.

4. Rachel is the networking administrator for a medium-sized organization that has a number of DNS servers. She has installed a new DNS server. This new server resolves host names for the current domain but does not resolve names in other domains. What must Rachel do to correct this problem?

a. Copy the zone files from the other domains.

b. Configure the root hints to the other servers.

c. Configure the authoritative servers for the other servers.

d. Configure automatic propagation from the other servers.

LAB 7.2 CONFIGURING THE DNS SERVER SERVICE

Objective

The goal of this lab is to configure a secondary zone for a DNS server.

Materials Required

This lab will require the following:

- STUDENT1 and STUDENT2 server access

- Completion of Lab 7.1

7

Estimated completion time: **15 minutes**

Activity Background

Secondary zones provide a read-only copy of the Primary DNS database. This provides added availability and fault tolerance when resolving name queries. If a single server is used and that server is not responding, queries for names in the zone can fail.

Activity

1. Return to the STUDENT1 server.

2. To open the DNS console, click **Start**, point to **Administrative Tools**, and then click **DNS**.

3. To configure the zone transfer properties for the forward lookup zone, expand **STUDENT1** in the console tree, expand **Forward Lookup Zones**, expand **domain1.classroom.com**, click **domain1.classroom.com**, click **Action** on the menu bar, click **Properties**, click the **Zone Transfers** tab, click the **Allow zone transfers** check box to select it, click the **Only to the following servers** option button, type **192.168.1.2** in the IP address text box, and then click **Add**.

4. To configure update notification, click **Notify**, click the **The following servers** option button, type **192.168.1.2** in the IP address text box, click **Add**, click **OK**, click **Apply**, and then click **OK**.

5. To create the reverse lookup zone, click **Reverse Lookup Zones** in the console tree, Click the **Action** menu, click **New Zone**, click **Next** three times, type **192.168.1** in the Network ID text box, click **Next** two times, review the summary, and then click **Finish**.

6. To configure the zone transfer properties for the reverse lookup zone, expand **Reverse Lookup Zones** in the console tree, click **192.168.1.x Subnet**, click **Action** on the menu bar, click **Properties**, click the **Zone Transfers** tab, click the **Allow zone transfers** check box to select it, click the **Only to the following servers** option button, type **192.168.1.2** in the IP address text box, and then click **Add**.

7. To configure update notification, click **Notify**, click the **The following servers** option button, type **192.168.1.2** in the IP address text box, click **Add**, click **OK**, click **Apply**, and then click **OK**.

8. Remain logged onto the STUDENT1 server with the DNS console open.

9. Return to the STUDENT2 server.

10. To launch the DNS console, click **Start**, point to **Administrative Tools**, and then click **DNS**.

11. To configure the DNS server root hint, click **STUDENT2** in the console tree, click the **Action** menu, click **Properties**, click the **Root Hints** tab, click **Add**, type **student1.domain1.classroom.com**, in the **Server fully qualified domain name (FQDN):** text box, click the **Resolve** button, click the **OK** button, click the **Apply** button, and then click the **OK** button.

12. To initiate the DNS server configuration, expand **STUDENT2** in the console tree, click the **Action** menu, click **Configure a DNS Server**, click **Next**, click the **Create forward and reverse lookup zones** option button, and then click **Next** twice.

13. To establish the forward secondary zone, click the **Secondary zone** option button, click **Next**, type **domain1.classroom.com** in the Zone name text box, click **Next**, type **192.168.1.1** in the IP address text box, click **Add**, and then click **Next** twice.

14. To establish the reverse secondary zone, click **Secondary zone** option button, click **Next**, click in the Network ID text box, type **192.168.1**, verify that **1.168.192.in-addr.arpa** appears in the Reverse lookup zone name text box, and then click **Next**.

15. To establish the master DNS server, type **192.168.1.1** in the IP address text box, click **Add**, click **Next** twice, click **Cancel** to abort the root hints search, review the summary of DNS settings that will be saved, click **Finish**, and then click **OK** to the root hints error message. The zone transfer is now completed.

16. To transfer the primary zone file, expand **Forward Lookup Zones** in the console tree, click **domain1.classroom.com**, click the **Action** menu, and then click **Transfer from Master**.

17. Remain logged on to the STUDENT2 server with the DNS console open.

Certification Objectives

Objectives for Microsoft Exam #70-291: Implementing, Managing, and Maintaining a Microsoft Windows Server 2003 Network Infrastructure:

- Install and configure the DNS Server Service

- Manage DNS

REVIEW QUESTIONS

7

1. Which of the following zones can you configure on a Windows Server 2003 DNS server? (Choose all that apply.)

   a. Standard Secondary

   b. Reverse Primary

   c. Primary Active Directory

   d. Standard Primary

   e. Active Directory Integrated

   f. Secondary Active Directory

2. Sally and Stu are discussing a DNS server design problem for a course at CyberU. CompanyA has a network of 2,500 computers with four DNS servers. They have one large DNS zone. CompanyA wants to distribute traffic loads among the servers and improve the performance of their DNS servers. Which of the following actions should CompanyA take?

   a. Place all of the DNS servers on the same subnet.

   b. Install one more DNS server.

   c. Purchase a switch and place the DNS servers behind the switch.

   d. Divide the single zone into multiple smaller zones.

3. Norma is tasked with installing multiple DNS servers for her network. She creates the following design goals for the DNS servers in her network:

   1. Fault tolerance for the primary DNS

   2. Minimize network traffic to replicate and synchronize zones

   3. Redundancy for DNS client queries

   Norma's project plan calls for the installation of the first Windows Server 2003 domain controller with an Active Directory integrated DNS. On the member server, she installs DNS Server Service and configures a secondary zone with the address of the first domain controller. Which of Norma's design goals are realized?

   a. Goal number 1

   b. Goal number 2

   c. Goal number 3

   d. None of the goals

LAB 7.3 CONFIGURING DNS ZONES

Objective

The goal of this lab is to create a forward lookup zone and a reverse lookup zone. In addition, you will create DNS resource records.

Materials Required

This lab will require the following:

- STUDENT1 and STUDENT2 server access

- Completion of Labs 7.1 and 7.2

Estimated completion time: **20 minutes**

Activity Background

Forward lookup zones provide a mechanism to resolve host names to IP addresses. Reverse lookup zones do the opposite: resolve an IP address to a host name. Both zones are useful for the configuration of DNS servers.

Activity

1. Return to the STUDENT1 server with the DNS console open.

2. To start the New Zone Wizard, expand **STUDENT1** in the DNS console, click **Forward Lookup Zones**, click the **Action** menu, click **New Zone**, and then click **Next**.

3. To create a new primary zone, verify that the **Primary zone** option button is selected, click **Next** twice, type **primary.domain1.classroom.com** in the Zone name text box, click **Next** twice, and then click **Finish**.

To delete an existing reverse lookup zone, expand **Reverse Lookup Zones**, right-click **192.168.1.X Subnet**, click **Delete**, and then click the **Yes** button twice.

NOTE

4. To start the New Zone Wizard, click **Reverse Lookup Zones**, click the **Action** menu, click **New Zone**, and then click the **Next** button.

5. To create the reverse lookup zone, verify that the **Primary zone** option button is selected, click **Next** twice, click in the Network ID text box, and then type **192.168.1**. Note that the name for the reverse lookup zone name, **1.168.192.in-addr.arpa**, has been entered. Click **Next** twice, review the summary, and then click **Finish**.

6. To manually add a host record, click **Forward Lookup Zones** in the console tree, click **primary.domain1.classroom.com** in the console tree, click the **Action** menu, click **New Host (A)**, type **STUDENTX12** in the Name (use parent domain name if blank) text box, click in the IP address text box, type **192.168.1.122**, click the **Add Host** button, click **OK**, and then click **Done**.

7. To verify that the host record was added to the forward lookup zone, click **primary.domain1.classroom.com** in the console tree, and then locate the Host record in the right pane to verify that the record was added.

8. To manually add a pointer (PTR) record, click **Reverse Lookup Zones** in the console tree, click **192.168.1.x Subnet** in the console tree, click the **Action** menu, click **New Pointer (PTR)**, type **122** in the Host IP number text box, click in the Host name text box, type **STUDENTX12**, and then click **OK**.

9. To verify that the pointer (PTR) record was added to the reverse lookup zone, click **192.168.1.x Subnet** in the console tree, and then locate the pointer (PTR) record in the right pane to verify that the record was added.

10. Remain logged on to the STUDENT1 server with the DNS console open.

Certification Objectives

Objectives for Microsoft Exam #70-291: Implementing, Managing, and Maintaining a Microsoft Windows Server 2003 Network Infrastructure:

- Install and configure the DNS Server Service

- Manage DNS

REVIEW QUESTIONS

1. What types of zones can be created in DNS? (Choose all that apply.)

   a. Forward zone lookup

   b. Host–to–IP zone

   c. Reverse zone lookup

   d. IP–to–host zone

2. You are the network administrator for the Catfish is Good chain of fast food restaurants. You have added a new database server to your Windows Server 2003 network. The application developers complain that they cannot access the new server by the name of CatfishData. However, they can access the database server by the IP address of 192.168.33.65. What do you do to solve the problem?

   a. Have the application developers create an entry in the hosts file on each development computer.

   b. Create an entry in the hosts file on the CatfishData server.

   c. Create a reserve entry on DHCP for the CatfishData server.

   d. Create a Host (A) record on the DNS server for the CatfishData server.

3. Having solved the Catfish data problem, you want to ensure that the new e-mail server installs without a problem. What kind of record will you add for the new e-mail server in DNS?

   a. EX

   b. MX

   c. PTR

   d. CNAME

   e. MAIL

4. You get a call from the application developers late on Friday afternoon. For security purposes, the developers want to be able to verify the host name for a given IP address. What kind of records will you need to add to the DNS?

    a. EX

    b. MX

    c. PTR

    d. CNAME

    e. MAIL

5. It is only six days until the developers release their new application to the various fast food restaurants. Their supervisor has reacted negatively to the name of the CatfishData server. He wants it to be known with an alternate name. He wants the name to be BigCat. What kind of record will you add to take care of the supervisor's request?

    a. EX

    b. MX

    c. PTR

    d. CNAME

    e. MAIL

7

Lab 7.4 Testing the DNS Server Service

Objective

The goal of this lab is to test the DNS service's ability to perform DNS queries.

Materials Required

This lab will require the following:

- STUDENT1 server access, as described in the lab setup section in the front of this lab manual.

- Completion of Labs 7.1 through 7.3

Estimated completion time: **15 minutes**

Activity Background

As a network administrator, you will need to test the DNS Server Service to determine whether the DNS server can resolve host names. It's always good to know the server's capabilities before network problems occur, or you will find yourself without a functional DNS. You have two basic tools available: the query test within DNS and the nslookup command.

Activity

1. Verify that you are logged on to the STUDENT1 server.

2. To perform a simple query against the DNS server, click **STUDENT1** in the console tree, click the **Action** menu, click **Properties**, click the **Monitoring** tab, click the **A simple query against this DNS server** check box to select it, and then click **Test Now**.

3. To clear the simple query, clear the **A simple query against this DNS server** check box, and then click **Cancel**.

4. To add a pointer (PTR) record for the first name server, click **Reverse Lookup Zones**, click **192.168.1.x Subnet** in the console tree, click the **Action** menu, click **New Pointer (PTR)**, type **1** in the Host IP number text box, click in the Host name text box, type **STUDENT1**, and then click **OK**.

5. To add a pointer (PTR) record for the second name server, expand **Reverse Lookup Zones**, click **192.168.1.x Subnet** in the console tree, click the **Action** menu, click **New Pointer (PTR)**, type **2** in the Host IP number text box, click in the Host name text box, type **STUDENT2**, and then click **OK**.

6. To start nslookup in interactive mode, click **STUDENT1**, click **Action** on the menu bar, and then click **Launch nslookup**.

To test a DNS server from another computer, you can start nslookup interactively by typing nslookup at a command prompt.

TIP

7. To locate the host record for a computer, type **set type=a**, press **Enter**, type **student1**, and then press **Enter**.

8. To locate the SOA record for a computer, type **set type=soa**, press **Enter**, type **student1**, and then press **Enter**.

9. To exit nslookup, type **exit**, and then press **Enter**.

10. Close the Command Prompt window.

11. Remain logged onto the STUDENT1 server with the DNS console open.

Certification Objectives

Objectives for Microsoft Exam #70-291: Implementing, Managing, and Maintaining a Microsoft Windows Server 2003 Network Infrastructure:

- Install and configure the DNS Server Service

- Manage DNS

- Monitor DNS

REVIEW QUESTIONS

7

1. Coleen is a network administrator for a Windows Server 2003 network. She has configured a DNS name server for the network and wants to test it. Which of the following might she do?

   a. At the Console tree, open the Properties dialog box for the server, and then click the Monitoring tab.

   b. At the command prompt, type nslookup to enter nslookup interactive mode.

   c. Use the DNS Server on the Administrative Tools menu.

   d. Use the NS Audit Wizard.

2. You use nslookup to test a DNS server, but the nslookup does not seem to work properly. You get a message that states that the name of the DNS server can not be found. Which of the following might be the reason?

   a. There is no host resource record for the DNS server.

   b. The computer that you want to locate was specified by a host name rather than an IP address.

   c. There is no pointer (PTR) record for the DNS server.

   d. The name of the DNS server was omitted in the nslookup syntax.

3. You are at a remote office resolving a problem assigned by the Helpdesk. After working through your standard troubleshooting process, you decide that there is possibly a missing host record on the DNS. What tools can you use from the remote office to verify your hunch?

   a. nslookup from DNS console

   b. nslookup from command prompt

   c. nscheck from DNS console

   d. nscheckfrom command prompt

Use the following information to answer Questions 4 and 5.

```
Default Server:   DNS1
Address:   192.168.110.1
> set type=a
> bangkok
Server:   DNS1
Address:   192.168.110.1
Name:     bangkok.orient.com
Address:   192.168.110.26
```

4. On which domain does the bangkok server reside?

   a. DNS1

   b. 192.168.110.1

   c. orient.com

   d. bangkok.orient.com

5. What query was made by nslookup to the DNS server?

   a. What is the host name for the 192.168.110.1 server?

   b. What is the IP address of the bangkok.orient.com server?

   c. What is the host name for the 192.168.110.26 server?

   d. What is the IP address of the DNS1.orient.com server?

Lab 7.5 Managing Dynamic Update

Objective

The goal of this lab is to configure a DNS zone for dynamic updates.

Materials Required

This lab will require the following:

- STUDENT1 and STUDENT2 server access

- Completion of Labs 7.1 through 7.4

7

Estimated completion time:**30 minutes**

Activity Background

You use the Dynamic Update feature to permit computers that run Windows 2000/XP to dynamically update the DNS zone database.

Activity

1. Verify that you are logged on to the STUDENT1 server with the DNS console open.

2. To open the DNS properties page, expand **Forward Lookup Zones** in the console tree, right-click **domain1.classroom.com** in the console tree, and then click **Properties**.

3. To setup DNS zones for dynamic updates, click the **General** tab, click the **Dynamic updates** drop-down list, click **Secure only**, click **Apply**, and then click **OK**.

4. Remain logged onto the STUDENT1 server with the DNS console open.

5. Return to the STUDENT2 server with the DNS console open.

6. To open a Command Prompt window, click **Start**, and then click **Command Prompt**.

7. To force a dynamic update to register with DNS, type **ipconfig /registerdns** at the command prompt, and then press **Enter**.

8. Wait 15 minutes. (This might be a good time to dream about that new computer you want to buy!)

9. Close the **Command Prompt** window.

10. To refresh Event Viewer, expand **Event Viewer** in the console tree, click **DNS Events**, click the **Action** menu, and then click **Refresh**.

11. Review the DNS Server event log for any errors.

12. Remain logged on to the STUDENT2 server with the DNS console open.

13. Return to the STUDENT1 server with the DNS console open for the next lab.

Certification Objectives

Objectives for Microsoft Exam #70-291: Implementing, Managing, and Maintaining a Microsoft Windows Server 2003 Network Infrastructure:

- Install and configure the DNS Server Service

- Manage DNS

REVIEW QUESTIONS

1. George would like to implement dynamic updates for his Windows Server 2003 servers. He establishes the following project goals:

   - Dynamic registration for computers with Windows XP Professional

   - Dynamic registration for computers with Linux

   - Dynamic registration for computers with Microsoft Windows ME

   George plans to allow dynamic updates for each of the zones in his DNS. In addition, he has no plans to configure his DHCP service to act as a proxy for down-level clients. Which of George's project goals are realized?

   a. Goal number 1

   b. Goal number 2

   c. Goal number 3

   d. None of the goals

2. Which of the following items about DNS dynamic updates is true?

   a. by default, allows the DHCP client computer to update host records

   b. Windows XP client computers update DNS servers without intervention by administrators

   c. by default, allows the DHCP client computer to update the mail record

   d. by default, allows the DHCP client computer to update the SOA record

   e. DNS can be configured to permit all operating systems to do dynamic updates.

3. You dozed off in class when Professor Boswell covered DNS dynamic update. So, when you installed your Windows Server 2003 network, you entered an A-record for each of your servers rather than using dynamic update. You get a call on your cell phone at lunch. It's Bob! He has added two new servers to your network. He stated that he tested the server by pinging by name which did not work. However, he stated that the ping using an IP address works. What will you tell Bob to do?

a. Run dcpromo on one of the new servers.

b. Use nslookup to verify that the DNS server is functioning.

c. Configure the Allow Dynamic Update setting as Secure.

d. Start and stop the DNS service.

7

LAB 7.6 MONITORING DNS PERFORMANCE

Objective

The goal of this lab is to monitor the performance of your DNS server.

Materials Required

This lab will require the following:

- STUDENT1 and STUDENT2 server access

- Completion of Labs 7.1 through 7.5

Estimated completion time: **20 minutes**

Activity Background

Why is DNS name resolution good? Well, consider that most users prefer a friendly name such as *www.course.com* to locate a Web server on a network rather than an IP address of 199.95.72.8. Quite simply, the friendly name is easier to learn and remember. So, when computers communicate over a network, DNS provides a way to map the user-friendly name of a computer to its numeric IP address. If you have ever used Microsoft Internet Explorer to surf the World Wide Web, you have used DNS.

Activity

1. Verify that you are logged on to the STUDENT1 server.

2. To launch Performance Monitor, click **Start**, point to **Administrative Tools**, and then click **Performance**.

3. To select Counter Logs, expand **Performance Logs and Alerts** in the console tree, and then click **Counter Logs**.

4. To initiate the creation of the DNS baseline, click **Action** on the menu bar, click **New Log Settings**, type **Baseline** in the Name text box, and then click **OK**.

5. To select the DNS Performance object DNS counters, click **Add Counters**, and then click **DNS** in the Performance object drop-down list.

6. To measure the query processing, scroll and click **Dynamic Update Received/sec** in the Select counters from list, and then click **Add**.

To view an explanation about each counter, click Explain.

TIP

7. To measure dynamic update activity, scroll and click **Total Query Received/sec** in the Select counters from list, and then click **Add**.

8. To select the Processor Performance object, scroll and click **Processor** in the Performance object drop-down list.

9. To measure processor utilization, scroll and click **%Processor Time** in the Select counters from list, click **Add**, and then click **Close**.

To remember the sequence to select a counter, think COCI: Computer, Object, Counter, Instance.

TIP

10. To increase the sampling rate, change the value in the Interval box to **5**, click **Apply**, click **Yes** to create a folder if necessary, and then click **OK**.

In a production environment, you would sample data over a longer period of time.

NOTE

11. Verify that the symbol next to Baseline in the right pane is green. Contact your instructor if the symbol is not green.

12. Wait several minutes for entries to be accumulated in the log.

13. To stop the logging, right-click **Baseline** in the right pane, and then click **Stop**.

14. To view the log in System Monitor, click **System Monitor** in the Performance console tree, click the disk drive symbol (fourth icon on the toolbar), click the **Log files** option button, click **Add,** click **Local Disk (C:)** in the Look in drop-down list, double-click **PerfLogs**, click the entry that resembles **Baseline_0000000.blg,** click the **Open** button, click **Apply**, and then click **OK**.

15. View the chart in System Monitor.

16. Close any open windows and shut down the STUDENT1 server.

17. Return to the STUDENT2 server, close any open windows, and shut down the STUDENT2 server.

Certification Objectives

Objectives for Microsoft Exam #70-291: Implementing, Managing, and Maintaining a Microsoft Windows Server 2003 Network Infrastructure:

- Monitor DNS

7

REVIEW QUESTIONS

1. You install the DNS service on a computer running Windows Server 2003. You want to determine the number of DNS requests submitted to the DNS server. What utility will you use to collect this information?

   a. Network monitor

   b. DNS request monitor

   c. System monitor

   d. DNS console

2. It has been a very busy morning! You suspect that a large number of Windows 2000/2003 computers have registered dynamic entries to the DNS server. You start up system monitor. What counter will you add for these dynamic registrations?

   a. %Processor time

   b. Dynamic updates received/sec

   c. Total query received/sec

   d. Bytes total/sec

3. You want to add an additional counter that will measure the number of requests for host name resolution. What counter will you add for these hostname resolutions?

   a. %Processor time

   b. Dynamic updates received/sec

   c. Total query received/sec

   d. Bytes total/sec

4. You anticipate that Professor Boswell will ask a question about System Monitor on the chapter quiz next class. You discuss the System Monitor counter dialog box with Ralph. Which of the following does Ralph give as the correct sequence to set up counters?

   a. object, counter

   b. object, counter, instance

   c. computer, object, counter, instance

   d. computer, object, instance

5. You need to run a log file to collect information on DNS activity, which you will compare to your previous baseline information. When you open System Monitor, you notice that the Baseline icon is red. What must you do to activate the Baseline log to capture additional information?

   a. Click the refresh button.

   b. Click the action menu, and click start.

   c. Click the start button.

   d. Click the action menu, and click restart.

IMPLEMENTING AND MANAGING
WINS

Labs included in this chapter:

- ◆ Lab 8.1 Installing WINS
- ◆ Lab 8.2 Configuring a WINS Server
- ◆ Lab 8.3 Managing WINS Records
- ◆ Lab 8.4 Configuring WINS Replication
- ◆ Lab 8.5 Maintaining a WINS Database

Microsoft MCSE Exam #70-291 Objectives	
Objective	Lab
Install and configure WINS service	8.1, 8.2, 8.3, 8.4
Manage WINS	8.3, 8.4, 8.5

LAB 8.1 INSTALLING WINS

Objective

The goal of this lab is to install the WINS (Windows Internet Name Service).

NOTE Although there are no direct questions on the Microsoft MCSE exam, WINS is required to manage legacy Windows computers. In addition, WINS can be integrated into DNS for resolution of host names that are not registered in DNS. For these reasons, a chapter on WINS is included in this lab manual.

Materials Required

This lab will require the following:

- STUDENT1 and STUDENT2 server access

- The Windows Server 2003 Installation CD-ROM

Estimated completion time: **30 minutes**

Activity Background

WINS provides a dynamic replicated database service to register and resolve NetBIOS computer names into IP addresses used on your network. After you install WINS on your server, your server acts as a NetBIOS name server to register and resolve computer or NetBIOS names for WINS-enabled client computers on your network.

Activity

1. Logon to the STUDENT1 server as **administrator** with the password **secret**.

2. Insert the Microsoft Windows Server 2003 CD-ROM. When the Microsoft Windows Server 2003 family window is displayed, click the **Exit** Hyperlink.

3. To open Add or Remove Programs, click **Start**, point to **Control Panel**, and then click **Add or Remove Programs**.

4. To install WINS, click the **Add/Remove Windows Components** icon, locate and click **Networking Services** (the label and not the check box), click **Details**, click the **Windows Internet Name Service (WINS)** check box to select it, click **OK**, click **Next**, wait for the files to copy and the configuration to complete, and then click **Finish**.

5. Close the Add or Remove Programs window.

6. To open the WINS console, click **Start**, point to **Administrative Tools**, and then click **WINS**.

7. To view the WINS server status, click **Server Status** in the console tree, and then verify that the status in the right pane displays **Responding**.

8. To view WINS Server Statistics, click **STUDENT1 [192.168.1.1]** in the console tree, click the **Action** menu, click **Display Server Statistics**, view the description and accompanying details, click **Refresh**, click **Reset**, and then click **Close**.

9. Remain logged on with the WINS console open.

10. Repeat Steps 1 through 9 for the STUDENT2 server.

Certification Objectives

Objectives for Microsoft Exam #70-291: Implementing, Managing, and Maintaining a Microsoft Windows Server 2003 Network Infrastructure:

■ Install and configure WINS

8

REVIEW QUESTIONS

1. Mike and Trina discuss name resolution for Windows Server 2003 networks. They ask you to summarize the methods that are used by Windows Server 2003 to resolve names to IP addresses. Which of the following will you include in your discussion? (Choose all that apply.)

   a. WINS resolves host names to IP addresses.

   b. Reverse WINS resolves IP addresses to network names.

   c. WINS resolves NetBIOS names to IP addresses.

   d. DNS resolves NetBIOS names to IP addresses.

   e. DNS resolves IP addresses to host names.

   f. WINS registers host names.

   g. DNS registers host names.

   h. WINS registers NetBIOS names.

2. You review the configuration for name resolution on a computer running Windows Server 2003. You discover that the computer is not configured to use the lmhosts file. However, the computer is configured to use the host file and DNS server. What steps does the computer take, and in what order, to resolve NetBIOS names?

   1. Client checks to see if the name queried is its local NetBIOS computer name

   2. Client broadcasts the NetBIOS query to the local subnet

   3. Client checks its local NetBIOS name cache of remote names

   4. Client checks the lmhosts file for a match to the query

   5. Client tries the Hosts file and then a DNS server

   6. Client forwards the NetBIOS query to its configured secondary WINS server

   7. Client forwards the NetBIOS query to its configured primary WINS server

   a. 1, 3, 7, 6, 2, 4, 5

   b. 1, 3, 7, 6, 2, 5

   c. 3, 7, 6, 2, 5

   d. 3, 7, 6, 2, 4, 5

3. You need to install the WINS service on your Windows Server 2003. What do you need to do?

   a. Launch the Install WINS Wizard.

   b. Insert the Windows Server 2003 CD-ROM, run Windows Server 2003 Setup, select ADD NETWORK Components, and then install WINS.

   c. Open the Control Panel, and then open Add/Remove Programs.

   d. Open the MMC, click the Action menu, and then select Install.

4. You are thinking out loud as you open the WINS console. You state that there must be someway to verify that the WINS server is working. Bob overhears your mutterings. What will Bob suggest that you do to view the current information regarding WINS operations?

   a. From a command prompt, run winstat.

   b. From the WINS console, expand the server icon.

   c. From the Action menu, select Display Server Statistics.

   d. Professor Boswell has not lectured on this topic.

LAB 8.2 CONFIGURING WINS

Objective

The goal of this lab is to configure the WINS server. As a network administrator, you make decisions regarding the performance of your WINS server. Among these decisions are server configuration parameters that determine how NetBIOS name records are managed in the WINS server database.

Materials Required

This lab will require the following:

- STUDENT1 and STUDENT2 server access

- Completion of Lab 8.1

8

Estimated completion time: **15 minutes**

Activity Background

Table 8-1 depicts the default, minimum, and maximum settings that can be applied for database records. In most cases, Microsoft recommends using the default values. In some cases, you might modify the defaults to accommodate special circumstances, such as when a host name change must be made or when you subnet your network so that hosts use different IP addresses.

Table 8-1 WINS Configuration Intervals

Interval	Description	Minimum	Default	Maximum
Renew Interval	How often a client renews registration of its names	40 minutes	6 days/144 hours	365 days
Extinction Interval	Interval between when an entry is marked as Released and when it is marked as Extinct in the WINS database	40 minutes	Depends on Renew interval	365 days
Extinction Timeout	Interval between when an entry is marked as Extinct and when it is scavenged from the WINS database	24 hours	Depends on Renew interval	365 days
Verification Interval	Period after which the WINS server must verify that old names that it does not own are still active	24 days	Depends on Renew interval	365 days

Activity

1. Verify that you are on the STUDENT1 server with the WINS console open.

2. To view the WINS intervals, click **STUDENT1 [192.168.1.1]** in the console tree, click the **Action** menu, click **Properties**, and then click the **Intervals** tab.

3. To configure the renew interval, decrease the value for the Renew interval: Days setting to **5**, and then click **Apply**.

4. To configure Enable burst handling, click the **Advanced** tab, click the **Low** option button, and then click **Apply**.

5. To configure for database verification, click the **Database Verification** tab, click the **Verify database consistency every** check box to select it, increase value for the Begin verifying at: Hours setting to **1**, click **Apply**, and then click **OK**.

6. Remain logged on to the STUDENT1 server with the WINS console open.

Certification Objectives

Objectives for Microsoft Exam #70-291: Implementing, Managing, and Maintaining a Microsoft Windows Server 2003 Network Infrastructure:

■ Install and configure WINS

REVIEW QUESTIONS

1. Your organization sets up a network with 2,250 clients. Because this is a new installation, all servers have Windows Server 2003 installed. The clients are a mixture of Windows 9x computers and Windows 2000 Professional computers. No Linux computers will be added to the network. What is the minimum number of WINS servers you should install? Why?

   a. 0, because WINS is needed only when Linux computers are added to the network

   b. 1, because a single WINS server can support up to 10,000 clients

   c. 2, to provide for fault tolerance

   d. 3, because a single WINS server is restricted to 1,000 clients

2. You create a new subnet and move 200 workstations from the old subnet to the new subnet. You want to ensure that the NetBIOS registrations are handled expeditiously. Typically, each computer will require three WINS registration entries. You have been asked to review the burst mode settings that specify how many name registration and name refresh requests sent by WINS clients are processed normally before burst-mode handling is started. To which value will you set the burst mode?

   a. low

   b. medium

   c. high

   d. custom

3. You are the network administrator for a Windows Server 2003 network. Your network consists of a number of "legacy" operating systems, including Windows 98 and Windows NT. For the next three months, you will be migrating your existing Windows NT servers to Windows Server 2003. During the migration period, you would like to have the servers provide more frequent registrations. How will you accomplish this?

   a. Change the renewal interval to 30 days.

   b. Change the renewal interval to 4 hours.

   c. Change the extinction interval to 30 days.

   d. Change the extinction interval to 4 hours.

   e. This cannot be done in WINS.

8

4. Jessie asks you about the consistency checking that WINS performs to help maintain database integrity among the WINS servers in your network. To explain the process, you create a small example of records for your WINS-A server and your WINS-B server. The records are in Table 8-2 and Table 8-3.

Table 8-2   WINS-A (192.168.22.1)

Record Name	Version	Owner	Expiration
AUSPR001	1F1	192.168.22.1	7/20/2004 11:23:45 AM
AUSPR002	1F2	192.168.22.1	7/20/2004 11:34:45 AM
AUSPR003	1F3	192.168.22.1	7/20/2004 11:34:45 AM

Table 8-3   WINS-B (192.168.22.2)

Record Name	Version	Owner	Expiration
AUSPR002	1F1	192.168.22.2	7/22/2004 11:34:45 AM
AUSPR003	1F5	192.168.22.2	7/22/2004 11:34:46 AM

After you walk Jessie through the database verification process, which of the following records will be active in the WINS-A server database? (Note that the fields for the records are in the record name, version, owner, and expiration sequence.)

a. AUSPR001 1F1 192.168.22.1 7/20/2002 11:23:45 AM

b. AUSPR002 1F2 192.168.22.2 7/20/2002 11:34:45 AM

c. AUSPR003 1F3 192.168.22.2 7/20/2002 11:34:46 AM

d. AUSPR002 1F2 192.168.22.2 7/22/2002 11:34:45 AM

e. AUSPR003 1F5 192.168.22.2 7/22/2002 11:34:46 AM

LAB 8.3 MANAGING WINS RECORDS

Objective

The goal of this lab is to create a static mapping for a computer that is not running a WINS-client service, and thus, is unable to participate in WINS name registration. As a network administrator, you need to add NetBIOS name records for such clients.

Materials Required

This lab will require the following:

- STUDENT1 and STUDENT2 server access

- Completion of Labs 8.1 and 8.2

Estimated completion time:**15 minutes**

Activity Background

In general, use only static WINS mappings for computer names, not group names for computers that do not directly use WINS for name registration. During replication, static mappings can overwrite dynamic mappings on other WINS servers and can be difficult to remove from all servers once they are introduced into the replicated WINS environment.

Mapped name-to-address entries can be added to WINS in one of two ways:

- Dynamically, by WINS-enabled clients directly contacting a WINS server to register, release, or renew their NetBIOS names in the server database

- Manually, by an administrator using the WINS console or command-line tools to add or delete statically mapped entries in the server database

Static entries are useful only when you need to add a name-to-address mapping to the server database for a computer that does not directly use WINS. For example, a Linux server without Samba cannot register a NetBIOS name directly with a WINS server. Although this name might be added to and resolved from an lmhosts file or by querying a DNS server, you might consider using a static WINS mapping instead.

ACTIVITY

Activity

1. Verify that you are on the STUDENT1 server with the WINS console open.

2. To create a static mapping, click **STUDENT1 [192.168.1.1]** in the console tree, click **Active Registrations** in the right pane, click the **Action** menu, click **New Static Mapping**, and then type **T01UNIX30** in the Computer name text box. Click **Unique** in the Type drop-down list box, type **192.168.1.133** in the IP address text box, click **Apply**, and then click **Cancel**.

NOTE

You may not see the entries added to the right pane until you refresh the screen in Step 3.

TIP

Because each static mapping is added to the database when you click Add, you cannot abort the dialog box. Should you make an error, delete the mapping with errors and add a new one using the correct information.

3. To find the T01UNIX30 computer in the active registrations, expand **STUDENT1 [192.168.1.1]** in the console tree, click **Active Registrations** in the console tree, click the **Action** menu, click **Display Records**, click the **Filter records matching this Name pattern** check box to select it, click in the Filter records matching this Name pattern text box and type **T01UNIX30**, click **Find Now**, and then view the Record Name, Type, IP Address, and State fields in the right pane. You should see multiple entries for T01UNIX30: WorkStation, Messenger, and File Server. Scroll the right pane to the right to locate additional fields.

4. Remain logged onto the STUDENT1 server with the WINS console open.

Certification Objectives

Objectives for Microsoft Exam #70-291: Implementing, Managing, and Maintaining a Microsoft Windows Server 2003 Network Infrastructure:

■ Install and configure WINS

■ Manage WINS

REVIEW QUESTIONS

1. You administer a Windows 2000 network with a WINS server on the network. You have three computers that are unable to register with your WINS server. Which of the following will fix the described problem?

a. Rename the computers with 15-character names.

b. Add static mappings for the computers.

c. Stop and restart the WINS service.

d. Run Jetpack to repair the WINS database.

e. Scavenge the WINS database.

2. You are taking two night classes from Professor Boswell. In addition to the Windows Server 2003 Network class, you are taking UNIX/LINUX Operating Systems. You are working days as an administrator for a mixed network with Windows and UNIX computers. The UNIX computers just keep on chugging along. So you try to leave them for the more experienced administrators. Your users report that they cannot access resources on the UNIX boxes by using their NetBIOS names. You know that this has not been a problem in the past. You recall that you were told that the UNIX boxes run SAMBA. And from what Professor Boswell has assured you, UNIX boxes with SAMBA are capable of NETBIOS communication. What do you do to fix the problem and restore connectivity for your clients to the UNIX boxes?

   a. Install and configure the Microsoft WINS for UNIX WINS client on the UNIX servers.

   b. Install WINS on the UNIX servers. Remove it from the Windows servers.

   c. Create a static address for each of the UNIX computers on the WINS server.

   d. Create a reserved address for each of the UNIX computers on the WINS server.

3. You want to be able to efficiently add static entries to WINS for the "live" test in your server class. You jot down the steps from memory and ask Rupert to see if the steps are correct.

   1. Click the Action menu.

   2. Type the IP address.

   3. Click New Static Mapping.

   4. Type the computer name.

   5. Click Apply.

What will Rupert say are the correct steps to add a static entry to WINS?

   a. 1, 2, 3, 4, 5

   b. 1, 3, 4, 2, 5

   c. 1, 3, 2, 4, 5

   d. 1, 2, 3, 5, 4

8

4. You have just added a static record for a UNIX01 server on your WINS server. You look in the right-pane of the WINS console and do not see any WINS entries. You want to verify that the UNIX01 server was added. What must you do to display the UNIX01 entry from the Action menu?

   a. Click the Refresh button.

   b. Click the Find now button.

   c. Click Display records, and then click the Find Now button.

   d. Click Display records, type UNIX01, and then click the Find Now button.

LAB 8.4 MANAGING WINS REPLICATION

Objective

The objective of this lab is to configure WINS replication. As a network administrator, you configure WINS replication on WINS servers within your network so that your WINS servers can share NetBIOS name registrations.

Materials Required

This lab will require the following:

- STUDENT1 and STUDENT2 server access

- Completion of Labs 8.1 through 8.3

Estimated completion time: **15 minutes**

Activity Background

For replication to work, you configure each WINS server with the other WINS server as its replication partner. This ensures that a name registered with one WINS server is eventually replicated to all other WINS servers in the network. A replication partner can be added and configured as a pull partner, a push partner, or a push/pull partner. The push/pull partner type is the default configuration, and Microsoft recommends this type for use in most cases.

Activity

1. Verify that you are on the STUDENT1 server with the WINS console open.

2. To add a replication partner, click **Replication Partners** under STUDENT1 [192.168.1.1] in the console tree, click the **Action** menu, click **New Replication Partner**, type **192.168.1.2** in the WINS server text box, and then click **OK**.

3. Wait while the new replication partner is contacted.

4. To view the replication partner's properties, click the **Action** menu, click **Properties**, click the **Push Replication** tab, and then click the **Pull Replication** tab.

5. To configure push replication, click the **Push Replication** tab, type **3** in the Number of changes in version ID before replication text box, verify the **Use persistent connections for push replication partners** check box is selected, and then click **Apply**.

6. To configure pull replication, click the **Pull Replication** tab, set the Start time: Hours setting to **2**, set the Replication interval: Days setting to **1**, and then click **Apply**.

7. To review the enable automatic partner configuration (leaving the push/pull settings intact), click the **Advanced** tab, click the **Enable automatic partner configuration** check box to select it, review the displayed information, uncheck the **Enable automatic partner configuration** check box, and then click **Apply**.

8. To enable static mappings to be overwritten during replication, click the **General** tab, check the **Overwrite unique static mappings at this server (migrate on)** check box, click the **Apply** button, and then click the **OK** button.

9. To force replication between WINS servers, click **Replication Partners** in the console tree, click the **Action** menu, click **Replicate Now**, click **Yes**, and then click **OK**.

10. Close the WINS console, but remain logged onto the STUDENT1 server.

Certification Objectives

Objectives for Microsoft Exam #70-291: Implementing, Managing, and Maintaining a Microsoft Windows Server 2003 Network Infrastructure:

- Install and configure WINS

- Manage WINS

8

REVIEW QUESTIONS

1. Jacob plans a WINS replication strategy for his Windows Server 2003 Network. Here are his goals for his WINS strategy:

   1. For high-speed LAN connections, ensure that updates occur in a timely manner.

   2. For low-speed WAN connections, minimize the frequency of WINS updates.

   3. For non-WINS clients, provide registration information.

   Jacob plans to install the WINS service on a number of Windows Server 2003 servers. For the home-office Austin LANs, he will install WINS on AUSDC001 and AUSDC002. For the Dallas remote LAN, he will install WINS on DALDC001. For the replication, he will establish these relationships: AUSDC001 will be set to push to AUSDC002 when 1,000 version ID changes occur; AUSDC002 will be set to pull from AUSDC001 every two hours; AUSDC001 will be set to push to DALDC001 every 75,000 version ID changes, and DALDC001 will be set to pull from AUSDC001 every 24 hours at 3:00 AM.

   Which of Jacob's goals will be achieved? (Choose all correct answers.)

   a. goal number 1

   b. goal number 2

   c. goal number 3

   d. No goals are achieved.

2. You have set up two WINS servers on your organization's Windows Server 2003 network. You want the two WINS servers to replicate, but you want the WINS replication to be configured automatically. What will you do?

   a. Nothing. Automatic partner configuration is not supported.

   b. Use the Services console to enable automatic partner configuration.

   c. Nothing. Automatic partner configuration is the default.

   d. Use the WINS console to enable automatic partner configuration.

3. Which of the following statements are true about a pull partner?

   a. requests entries at a specified interval

   b. may increase network traffic

   c. does not maintain synchronization as well as a push partner

   d. notifies partners when a specified threshold is exceeded

4. Which types of links are more suitable for a pull partner when configuring WINS?

   a. slow links

   b. fast links

   c. fiber-optic links

   d. ATM links

5. You are the network administrator for a Windows Server 2003 network. You setup a pair of WINS servers to provide fault tolerance. Now you need to establish replication between the two WINS servers. What is the recommended setting if both servers are connected by local area networks?

   a. The first server is a pull partner and the second server is a push partner.

   b. Both servers are pull partners.

   c. Both servers are push partners.

   d. Both servers are PUSH/PULL partners.

8

LAB 8.5 MAINTAINING A WINS DATABASE

Objective

The objective of this lab is to maintain the WINS database. The WINS database uses a version of the Extensible Storage Engine, which serves both Microsoft Exchange and Windows Server 2003 Active Directory.

Materials Required

This lab will require the following:

- STUDENT1 and STUDENT2 server access

- Completion of Labs 8.1 through 8.4

Estimated completion time: **15 minutes**

Activity Background

The size of the WINS database grows as NETBIOS registrations occur. The database grows because, as entries are added and removed, the amount of space is not immediately returned; thus, you must take four actions to improve the performance of the WINS server.

The first action is Tombstoning deleted record(s) on a WINS server, which allows other WINS servers (when they replicate) to update their database properly.

The second action is scavenging, which occurs when the WINS server database deletes and removes obsolete information that remains after changes occur. Like any database, the WINS server database of address mappings needs to be periodically scavenged and backed up.

The third action is using the WINS backup tools to back up and restore the WINS database. After you specify a local backup folder for the database, WINS performs complete database backups by default every three hours, using the specified folder. In addition, you can configure to backup the database automatically when the service is stopped or the server computer shut down.

The fourth action comprises scheduling consistency checking to compare the WINS database entries on all the WINS servers. During these scheduled consistency checks, the specified WINS server compares local copies of its records with the same records stored at the WINS server listed as the owner for each record.

ACTIVITY

Activity

1. Verify that you are on the STUDENT2 server with the WINS console open.

2. To manually back up the database, click **STUDENT2 [192.168.1.2]** in the console tree, click the **Action** menu, click **Back Up Database**, expand **Local Disk (C:)**, expand **WINDOWS**, scroll and expand **system32**, scroll and click the **WINS** folder, click **OK**, read the WINS message, and then click **OK**.

3. To scavenge the WINS database, click **STUDENT2 [192.168.1.2]** in the console tree, click the **Action** menu, click **Scavenge Database**, review the WINS message, and then click **OK**.

4. To check WINS database consistency, click **STUDENT2 [192.168.1.2]** in the console tree, click the **Action** menu, click **Verify Database Consistency**, read the **WARNING** message, click **Yes**, review the WINS message, and then click **OK**.

5. To view the system log for WINS entries, click **Start**, click **Administrative Tools**, click **Event Viewer**, click **System** in the console tree, click the **View** menu, click **Filter**, scroll and click **WINS** in the Event source drop-down list, click **Apply**, and then click **OK**.

6. Review the WINS entries.

NOTE

You should disregard error messages that state "The description for Event ID.... cannot be found."

7. Close all open windows and shutdown the STUDENT2 server.

8. Return to the STUDENT1 server. Close all open windows and shutdown STUDENT1 server.

Certification Objectives

Objectives for Microsoft Exam #70-291: Implementing, Managing, and Maintaining a Microsoft Windows Server 2003 Network Infrastructure:

- Manage WINS

REVIEW QUESTIONS

1. You discover that your WINS database is not being automatically backed up. What steps should you take, and in what order, to correct the problem?

   1. Select your server, click the Action menu, and then click Properties.

   2. Create a folder and share the folder from another server.

   3. Create a folder on the local computer.

   4. Stop the WINS service.

   5. Specify the folder location in the Default backup path text box.

   6. Select Back up database during server shutdown.

   7. Wait three hours for the backup to occur.

   8. Verify that the backup files are present in a subfolder of the \Wins_bak\New folder.

   a. 1, 5, 8

   b. 1, 5

   c. 1, 2, 6, 8

   d. 1, 3, 6, 8

   e. 1, 3, 4, 6, 8

   f. 1, 3, 5, 6, 7, 8

2. You manage a Windows Server 2003 WINS server. You want to check the WINS database for consistency? What do you need to do?

   a. Use the WINSDB utility.

   b. Use the WINSCL utility.

   c. In the WINS console, click the Action menu, and then click Verify Database Consistency.

   d. Edit the registry to enable consistency checking, and then use the WINS console to check the WINS database consistency.

3. You manage a Windows 2003 Server with WINS installed on it. This WINS server replicates with another WINS server. As you review the records in the WINS console, you notice that three of the records have invalid IP addresses. What step should you take on your server to correct this problem on your WINS server?

   a. Delete the records.

   b. Tombstone the records.

   c. Run Verify Database Consistency.

   d. Restore the last WINS database.

4. You are the network administrator for a Windows Server 2003 network. Your WINS servers have been up and running for several months. They have been managing NetBIOS registrations for your 1250 legacy computers. Being a proactive administrator, you would like to know what you might do to maintain the efficiency of the WINS database. What would be a prudent course of action?

   a. Tombstone duplicate records.

   b. Verify database consistency.

   c. Filter the database.

   d. Scavenge the database.

9

SECURING NETWORK TRAFFIC

Labs included in this chapter:

♦ Lab 9.1 Implementing IPSec

♦ Lab 9.2 Testing IPSec

♦ Lab 9.3 Creating a Certificate Authority

♦ Lab 9.4 Creating an IP Security Policy

Microsoft MCSE Exam #70-291 Objectives	
Objective	Lab
Implement secure network administration procedures	9.1, 9.2, 9.3. 9.4
Monitor network protocol security	9.2, 9.4
Troubleshoot network protocol security	9.2, 9.3, 9.4

Lab 9.1 Implementing IPSec

Objective

The goal of this lab is to create a secure server using IPSec (Internet Protocol Security) to secure traffic between two servers. In this lab, you will configure the STUDENT2 server to act as a secure server. In the next lab, you will the use the STUDENT4 server to act as a client and test a secure connection to the STUDENT2 server.

Materials Required

This lab will require the following:

- STUDENT1 and STUDENT2 server access

Estimated completion time: **20 minutes**

Activity Background

The configuration of IPSec requires the installation of snap-ins for the MMC. In this lab, you will add the IP Security Monitor and IP Security Policy Management snap-ins to the MMC. You will be using the ping command in the next lab to test IP Security. This will require that you create a test policy with the IP Security Policy and a security rule for the ICMP traffic generated by the ping command.

ACTIVITY

Activity

1. Log on to the STUDENT2 server as **administrator** with the password **secret**.

2. To see whether STUDENT2 is a member of the Workgroup: WORKGROUP or the Domain: domain1.classroom.com, click **Start**, right-click **My Computer**, click **Properties**, click the **Computer Name** tab, click **Change**, and then verify the server is a member of the Workgroup: WORKGROUP. If the server is a member of the Workgroup: WORKGROUP, continue with Step 3; otherwise, continue with Step 5.

3. To make STUDENT2 a member of the domain1.classroom.com domain, click the **Domain** option button, click in the Domain text box, type **domain1.classroom.com**, click **OK**, type **administrator** in the User name text box, type **secret** in the Password text box, and then click **OK**.

4. When the "Welcome to the domain1.classroom.com domain." message appears, click **OK**. When the "You must restart the computer for the changes to take effect." message appears, click **OK**, and then click **OK** again. When the "Do you want to restart your computer now?" message appears, click **Yes**, and then go to Step 6.

5. To log off the server, click **Cancel** twice, click **Start**, click **Log Off**, and then click **Log Off**.

6. If the Logon to drop-down box is not displayed, click **Options**. Click the **Log on to** drop-down arrow, click **DOMAIN1**, click in the Password text box and type **secret**, and then click **OK**.

7. To open the MMC (Microsoft Management Console), click **Start**, click **Run**, type **mmc** in the Open list box, and then click **OK**.

8. To add the Computer Management snap-in, click the **File** menu, click **Add/Remove Snap-in**, click **Add**, scroll and click **Computer Management** in the Available Standalone Snap-ins list box, click **Add**, and then click **Finish**.

9. To add the IP Security Monitor snap-in, scroll and click **IP Security Monitor** in the Available Standalone Snap-ins list box, and then click **Add**.

10. To add the IP Security Policy Management snap-in, scroll and click **IP Security Policy Management** in the Available Standalone Snap-ins list box, click **Add**, click **Finish**, click **Close**, and then click **OK**.

11. To reduce the refresh value for the IP Security Monitor, expand **IP Security Monitor** in the console tree, expand **STUDENT2** in the console tree, right-click **STUDENT2** in the console tree, click **Properties**, type **1** in the Refresh interval seconds text box, click **Apply**, and then click **OK**.

NOTE
To avoid excessive system overhead in a production environment, you would not set the refresh seconds for the IP Security Monitor below a value of 15 seconds.

12. To create an IP security policy, click **IP Security Policies on Local Computer** in the console tree, click the **Action** menu, click **Create IP Security Policy**, click **Next**, type **Test Policy** in the Name text box, click **Next**, clear the **Activate the default response rule** check box, click **Next**, and then click **Finish**.

13. To create a security rule, click **Add**, click **Next** three times to accept the default values, click the **All ICMP Traffic** option button, click **Next**, click the **Require Security** option button, click **Next** twice, click **Finish**, and then click **OK** twice.

14. To assign the IP security policy, click **IP Security Policies on Local Computer** in the console tree, right-click **Test Policy** in the right pane, and then click **Assign**. Verify that the status in the Policy Assigned column changes to **Yes**.

15. To restart the IPSec Policy Agent, expand **Computer Management (Local)** in the console tree, expand **Services and Applications** in the console tree, click **Services** in the console tree, scroll and click **IPSEC Services** in the right pane, and then click the **Restart the service** hyperlink. If you receive the IP Security monitor error message, click **OK**.

16. To reconnect the IP Security Monitor, expand **IP Security Monitor** in the console tree, right-click **STUDENT2** in the console tree, and click **Reconnect**.

17. Remain logged onto the STUDENT2 server with the console open.

Certification Objectives

Objectives for Microsoft Exam #70-291: Implementing, Managing, and Maintaining a Microsoft Windows Server 2003 Network Infrastructure:

- Implement secure network administration procedures

REVIEW QUESTIONS

1. Jan and Bob are discussing IPSec. They ask you at what layer IPSec operates in the OSI model. How do you respond?

   a. Application layer

   b. Transport layer

   c. Network layer

   d. Physical layer

2. Bob wants to enable encrypted communications between members of the executive committee. He is concerned about e-mail being subject to eavesdropping. Bob would like to address these concerns without requiring existing e-mail clients to be replaced. What should Bob employ to address his concerns?

   a. IPSec

   b. Kerberos v5

   c. Smart Cards

   d. SSL

3. Allison and Robert are concerned about their IP packets that travel within the company network. They want to ensure the authenticity, integrity, and confidentiality of the data at the Transport layer. In addition, they want to protect the integrity of the IP header. Which of the IPSec protocols will they select to accomplish their objectives?

   a. AH protocol

   b. ESP protocol

   c. both AH and ESP protocols

   d. none of the above

4. IPSec is a set of Internet standards that uses cryptographic security services to provide which of the following? (Choose all that apply.)

a. Confidentiality

b. Compression

c. Authentication

d. Flow control

e. Data integrity

LAB 9.2 TESTING IPSEC

Objective

The goal of this lab is to test IPSec to secure traffic between two servers. In this lab, you will configure the STUDENT4 computer to act as a client and the STUDENT2 computer to act as a secure server. The client using the ping command will initially send unprotected ICMP echo packets to the server, but the server will request security from the client, after which the rest of the communication will be secure.

9

Materials Required

This lab will require the following:

- STUDENT1, STUDENT2, and STUDENT4 server access

- Completion of Lab 9.1

Estimated completion time: **25 minutes**

Activity Background

The environment to test IP Security requires that two servers be present in the same domain. To facilitate this testing, an additional server will be borrowed and added to the existing domain. As in the previous lab, you will add the IP Security Monitor and IP Security Policy Management snap-ins to the MMC for the borrowed server. This will require that you create a test policy with IP Security Policy Management and a security rule for the ICMP traffic generated by the ping command. To test for IP Security, you will issue a ping command. From the IP Security Monitor, you will view the details of the active security policy.

ACTIVITY

Activity

1. To connect the STUDENT4 server to the 192.168.1.0 segment, attach the data cable used by the STUDENT4 server to the same hub used by the STUDENT1 and STUDENT2 servers.

2. Log on to the STUDENT4 server as **administrator** with the password **secret**.

3. To configure the IP address for STUDENT4, click **Start**, point to **Control Panel**, point to **Network Connections**, click **Local Area Connection**, click **Properties**, click **Internet Protocol [TCP/IP]**, click **Properties**, record the IP address, click the **Use the following IP address** option button, type **192.168.1.4** in the IP address field, press **Tab** to allow Windows Server 2003 to fill in the default subnet mask of **255.255.255.0**, record the DNS Server IP address, type **192.168.1.1** as the Preferred DNS server address, click **OK**, and then click **Close** twice.

4. To see whether STUDENT4 is a member of the Workgroup: WORKGROUP or Domain: domain1.classroom.com, click **Start**, right-click **My Computer**, click **Properties**, click the **Computer Name** tab, click **Change**, and then verify the server is a member of the Workgroup: WORKGROUP. If the server is a member of the Workgroup: WORKGROUP continue with Step 5; otherwise, continue with Step 7.

5. To make STUDENT4 a member of the domain1.classroom.com domain, click the **Domain** option button, click in the Domain text box and type **domain1.classroom.com**, click **OK**, type **administrator** in the User name text box, type **secret** in the Password text box, and then click **OK**.

6. When the "Welcome to the domain1.classroom.com domain" message appears, click **OK**. When the "You must restart this computer for the changes to take effect" message appears, click **OK**, and then click **OK**. When the "Do you want to restart your computer now?" message appears, click **Yes** and then go to Step 8.

7. To log off from the server, click **Cancel** twice, click **Start**, click **Logoff**, and then click **Log off**.

8. If the Logon to drop-down box is not displayed, click **Options**. Click the **Log on to** drop-down arrow, click **DOMAIN1**, click in the Password text box and type **secret**, and then click **OK**.

9. To launch the MMC, click **Start**, click **Run**, type **mmc** in the Open text box, and then click **OK**.

10. To add the Computer Management snap-in, click the **File** menu, click **Add/Remove Snap-in**, click **Add**, scroll and click **Computer Management** in the Available Standalone Snap-ins list box, click **Add**, and then click **Finish**.

11. To add the IP Security Monitor, scroll and click **IP Security Monitor** in the Available Standalone Snap-ins list box, and then click **Add**.

12. To add the IP Security Policy Management snap-in, scroll and click **IP Security Policy Management** in the Available Standalone Snap-ins list box, click **Add**, and then click **Finish**, click **Close**, and then click **OK**.

13. To reduce the refresh value for the IP Security Monitor, expand **IP Security Monitor** in the console tree, expand **STUDENT4** in the console tree, right-click **STUDENT4** in the console tree, click **Properties**, type **1** in the Refresh interval seconds text box, click **Apply**, and then click the **OK** button.

14. To activate the built-in client policy on STUDENT4, click **IP Security Policies on Local Computer** in the console tree, right-click **Client (Respond Only)** in the right pane, and then click **Assign**. Verify that the status in the Policy Assigned column changes to **Yes**.

15. To restart the IPSec Policy Agent, expand **Computer Management (Local)** in the console tree, expand **Services and Applications** in the console tree, click **Services** in the console tree, scroll and click **IPSEC Services** in the right pane, and then click the **Restart the service** hyperlink. If you receive the IP Security monitor error message, click **OK**.

16. To reconnect the IP Security Monitor, expand **IP Security Monitor** in the console tree, right-click on **STUDENT4** in the console tree, and click **Reconnect**.

17. To open a command prompt, click **Start** and then click **Command Prompt**.

18. To verify that IPSec is being negotiated, type **ping 192.168.1.2 –w 100** at the command prompt, and then press **Enter**. Your output should resemble the following:

```
C:\Documents and Settings\Administrator.DOMAIN1>ping
192.168.1.2 —w 100

Pinging 192.168.1.2 with 32 bytes of data:

Negotiating IP Security.
Reply from 192.168.1.2: bytes=32 time<1ms TTL=128
Reply from 192.168.1.2: bytes=32 time<1ms TTL=128
Reply from 192.168.1.2: bytes=32 time<1ms TTL=128
Ping statistics for 192.168.1.2:
    Packets: Sent = 4, Received = 3, Lost = 1 (25% loss),
Approximate round trip times in milli-seconds:
    Minimum = 0ms, Maximum = 0ms, Average = 0ms
```

NOTE
You may need to execute the ping command several times. Press the Up-arrow key and press Enter to execute the ping command.

19. To view the details of the active policy, return to the MMC window, expand **IP Security Monitor** in the console tree, and then click **Active Policy** in the console tree.

20. To deactivate the policy on STUDENT4, click **IP Security Policies on Local Computer** in the console tree, right-click **Client (Respond Only)** in the right pane, and then click **Un-assign**. Verify that the status in the Policy Assigned column changes to **No**.

21. Remain logged on to the STUDENT4 server with the console and command prompt open.

22. To deactivate the policy on STUDENT2, go to the STUDENT2 server, click **IP Security Policies on Local Computer** in the console tree, right-click **Test Policy** in the right pane, and then click **Un-assign**.

23. Remain logged on the STUDENT2 server with the console open.

Certification Objectives

Objectives for Microsoft Exam #70-291: Implementing, Managing, and Maintaining a Microsoft Windows Server 2003 Network Infrastructure:

- Implement secure network administration procedures

- Monitor network protocol security

- Troubleshoot network protocol security

REVIEW QUESTIONS

1. You are testing IPSec communications in the lab at CyberU. You examine entries in the IP Security Monitor. You do not see an active policy in the IP Security Monitor. Which of the following can you configure to correct the problem?

   a. the event viewer service

   b. the Oakley service

   c. the policy agent

   d. an audit policy

2. You will be testing IPSec communications. Which of the available tools on your computer will you use to facilitate this testing? (Choose all that apply.)

a. Active Directory Users and Computers

b. IPSec driver sniffer

c. Oakley logger

d. ping command

e. IPSec Security Monitor

f. AH logger

g. ESP logger

3. Sheila will be testing IPSec and needs to create an MMC with the tools to facilitate the IPSec testing.

She establishes the following goals for her MMC:

1. Start or restart the IPSec service.

2. Assign an IPSec policy.

3. Reconnect the IPSec Monitor.

4. Open a command prompt window.

She launches the MMC and adds the Computer Management, IP Security Monitor and IP Security Management snap-ins.

Which of her goals will be met?

a. Goal 1

b. Goal 2

c. Goal 3

d. Goal 4

e. none of the goals

LAB 9.3 CREATING A CERTIFICATE AUTHORITY

Objective

The goal of this lab is to install Certificate Services and create an Enterprise Certificate Authority (CA). In this lab, you will establish an Enterprise root CA for the domain1. classroom.com.

Materials Required

This lab will require the following:

- STUDENT1 server access

- Completion of Labs 9.1 and 9.2

Estimated completion time:**15 minutes**

Activity Background

In this lab, you will set up an enterprise root certificate server. With this certificate server, you will be able to issue IP Security certificates that will be used to secure the packets transferred between the two servers. You will install Internet Information Server to use the Web-based application to request and install the certificates.

Activity

1. Log on to the STUDENT1 server as **administrator** with the password **secret**.

2. To start the Windows Component Wizard, click **Start**, point to **Control Panel**, click **Add or Remove Programs**, and then click **Add/Remove Windows Components**.

3. Insert the Microsoft Windows Server 2003 CD-ROM. When the Microsoft Windows Server 2003 family window is displayed, click the **Exit** hyperlink.

4. To install Internet Information Server (IIS), click **Application Server** (the label and not the check box), click **Details**, click **Internet Information Server (IIS)** (the label and not the check box), click **Details**, click the **Common Files** check box to select it, click the **Internet Information Services Manager** check box to select it, scroll and click the **World Wide Web Service** list box to select it, click **OK** twice, click **Next**, and then wait for the files to copy and the service to configure, and then click **Finish**.

5. To install Certificate Services, click **Add/Remove Windows Components**, click the **Certificate Services** check box to select it, click **Yes** to acknowledge the warning, and then click **Next**.

6. To set up the Enterprise root CA, verify the **Enterprise root CA** option button is selected, click **Next**, type **Classroom Enterprise CA** in the Common name for this CA text box, and then click **Next**. If necessary, click **Yes** to acknowledge the "The private key 'Classroom Enterprise CA' already exists. Do you want to overwrite this key with a new one?" message. Click **Next**, click **Yes** to temporarily stop the IIS, wait for IIS to stop, and then wait for Certificate Services to be configured.

For your organization, an appropriate certificate life might be about two years.

NOTE

7. Click **Yes** to enable Active Server Pages, wait for configuration to complete, click **Finish**, and then close the Add or Remove Programs window.

8. To create an MMC for certificate management, click **Start**, click **Run**, type **mmc** in the Open text box, click **OK**, click the **File** menu, click **Add/Remove Snap-in**, and then click **Add**.

9. To add the Certificates snap-in, click **Certificates** in the Available Standalone Snap-ins list box, click **Add**, click the **Computer account** option button, click **Next**, and then click **Finish**.

10. To add the Certification Authority snap-in, click **Certification Authority** in the Available Standalone Snap-ins list box, click **Add**, click the **Local Computer** option button, click **Finish**, click **Close**, and then click **OK**.

11. To establish the IPSec certificates, expand **Certification Authority (Local)** in the console tree, expand **Classroom Enterprise CA** in the console tree, click **Certificate Templates** in the console tree, click the **Action** menu, click **New**, click **Certificate Template to Issue**, scroll and click **IPSec**, click **OK**, click **Certificate Templates** in the console tree, click the **Action** menu, click **New**, click **Certificate Template to Issue**, scroll and click **IPSec (Offline request)**, and then click **OK**.

12. To view the certificates for the local computer, expand **Certificates (Local Computer)** in the console tree, click the **Action** menu, click **Refresh**, expand **Personal** in the console tree, and then double-click **Certificates** in the console tree. View the certificates in the right pane.

13. To view the certificate details, double-click **Classroom Enterprise CA** in the right pane, read the Certificate Information, click the **Details** tab, scroll and read the details, and then click the **OK** button.

14. Remain logged onto STUDENT1 with the console open. Return to the STUDENT2 server for the next lab.

Certification Objectives

Objectives for Microsoft Exam #70-291: Implementing, Managing, and Maintaining a Microsoft Windows Server 2003 Network Infrastructure:

- Implement secure network administration procedures

- Troubleshoot network protocol security

REVIEW QUESTIONS

1. You want to install an Enterprise CA on a Windows 2000 server. Which of the following are required?

    a. The computer where the CA is installed must use Active Directory.

    b. You must have write permission to Active Directory.

    c. DNS is required.

    d. You must have Enterprise Administrator privileges to the CA server.

    e. The computer in which the CA is installed must be a domain controller.

2. You have a bet with another worker about the PKI acronym. Based upon her response, you select a restaurant. What entree will you be eating tonight?

    a. hamburgers, as PKI stands for Public Key Infrastructure

    b. grilled chicken, as PKI stands for Packet Key Information

    c. salad, as PKI stands for Pretty Kid Infrastructure

    d. seafood, as PKI stands for Public Knowledge Information

3. You want to issue certificates to be used by IPSec. Which of the following are required? (Choose all that apply).

    a. IPSec stack expander

    b. Certificate Services

    c. IIS

    d. IPSec templates

    e. PKI templates

LAB 9.4 CREATING AN IP SECURITY POLICY

Objective

The goal of this lab is to create a security policy which obtains a certificate from the Enterprise Certificate Authority.

Materials Required

This lab will require the following:

- STUDENT1, STUDENT2, and STUDENT4 server access

- Completion of Labs 9.1 through 9.3

Estimated completion time: **45 minutes**

Activity Background

9

In this lab, you will use certificates to secure the packets transferred between two servers. You will request the certificates for the two servers using the certsrv web-based application. To enable IP Security, you create a IP security policy and a certificate policy for each server. With the ping command, you will test the IP security between the two servers. You will use the IP Security Monitor to view the details of IP security between the two servers. Lastly, you will return the borrowed server to its previous state.

Activity

1. Verify that you are on the STUDENT2 server with the console open.

2. If Internet Explorer Enhanced Security Configuration is enabled on your server, click **Start**, point to **Control Panel**, click **Add or Remove Programs**, click **Add/Remove Windows Components**, clear the **Internet Explorer Enhanced Security Configuration** check box, click **Next**, click **Finish**, and then close the Add or Remove Programs window. If not, continue with Step 3.

3. To display the Certificate Service Web page, click **Start**, point to **All Programs**, click **Internet Explorer**, type **http://student1/certsrv/** in the Address bar, and then press **Enter**.

4. To install the CA chain, click the **Download a CA certificate, certificate chain, or CRL** hyperlink, click the **install this CA certificate chain** hyperlink, click **Yes** when the security warning message appears, wait for the message indicating that the chain has been successfully installed, and then click **Back** twice.

5. To request a user certificate, click the **Request a certificate** hyperlink, click the **advanced certificate request** hyperlink, click the **Create and submit a request to this CA** hyperlink, click the **Certificate Template** pull-down arrow, and then click the **IPSec (Offline request)**.

6. To complete the Web submission form, type **Administrator** in the Name text box, type **admin@classroom.com** in the E-Mail text box, type **Course** in the Company text box, type **IT** in the Department text box, type *your city* in the City text box, type *your state* in the State text box. Under Key Options, click the **Store certificate in the local computer certificate store** check box to select it, and then scroll down the page and click the **Submit** button, and then click **Yes** to acknowledge the Potential Scripting Violation warning.

7. To install the user certificate, click the **Install this certificate** hyperlink, click **Yes** to acknowledge the Potential Scripting Violation warning, wait for the message indicating that the certificate has been successfully installed, and then close Internet Explorer.

8. To create an IP security policy, click **IP Security Policies on Local Computer** in the console tree, click the **Action** menu, click **Create IP Security Policy**, click **Next**, type **Certificate Policy** in the Name text box, click **Next**, clear the **Activate the default response rule** check box, click **Next**, and then click **Finish**.

9. To create an IP security rule, click **Add**, click **Next** three times to accept the defaults, click the **All ICMP Traffic** option button, click **Next**, click the **Require Security** option button, click **Next**, click the **Use a certificate from this certification authority (CA)** option button, click **Browse**, click the **Issued to** column heading button twice to sort the entries, expand the column to view the names, scroll and click **Classroom Enterprise CA**, click **OK**, click **Next**, click **Finish**, and then click **OK** twice.

10. To activate the certificate policy, click **IP Security Policies on Local Computer** in the console tree, right-click **Certificate Policy** in the right pane, and then click **Assign**. Verify that the status in the Policy Assigned column changes to **Yes**.

11. To restart the IPSec Policy Agent, expand **Computer Management** in the console tree, expand **Services and Applications** in the console tree, click **Services** in the console tree, scroll and click **IPSEC Services** in the right pane, and then click the **Restart the service** hyperlink. If you receive the IP Security Monitor error message, click **OK**.

12. To reconnect the IP Security Monitor, expand **IP Security Monitor** in the console tree, right-click on **STUDENT2** in the console tree, and click **Reconnect**.

13. Remain logged on to the STUDENT2 server with the console open.

14. Go to the STUDENT4 server.

15. If Internet Explorer Enhanced Security Configuration is enabled on your server, click **Start**, click **Control Panel**, click **Add or Remove Programs**, click **Add/Remove Windows Components**, clear the **Internet Explorer Enhanced Security Configuration** check box, click **Next** and then click **Finish**. Close the Add or Remove Programs window. If not, continue with Step 16.

16. To display the Certificate Service Web page, click **Start**, point to **All Programs**, click **Internet Explorer**, type **http://student1/certsrv/** in the Address bar, and then press the **Enter** key.

17. To install the CA chain, click the **Download a CA certificate, certificate chain, or CRL** hyperlink, click the **install this CA certificate chain** hyperlink, click the **Yes** button when the security warning message appears, wait for the message indicating that the chain has been successfully installed, and then click the **Back** button twice.

18. To request a user certificate, click the **Request a certificate** hyperlink, click the **advanced certificate request** hyperlink, click the **Create and submit a request to this CA** hyperlink, click the **Certificate Template** pull-down arrow, and then click the **IPSec (Offline request)**.

19. To complete the Web submission form, type **Administrator** in the Name text box, type **admin@classroom.com** in the E-Mail text box, type **Course** in the Company text box, type **IT** in the Department text box, type *your city* in the City text box, type *your state* in the State text box. Under Key Options: click the **Store certificate in the local computer certificate store** check box, and then click **Submit**, and then click **Yes** to acknowledge the Potential Scripting Violation warning.

20. To install the user certificate, click the **Install this certificate** hyperlink, click **Yes** to acknowledge the Potential Scripting Violation warning, wait for the message indicating that the certificate has been successfully installed, and then close Internet Explorer.

21. To create an IP security policy, click **IP Security Policies on Local Computer** in the console tree, click the **Action** menu, click **Create IP Security Policy**, click **Next**, type **Certificate Policy** in the Name text box, click **Next**, clear the **Activate the default response rule** check box, click **Next**, and then click **Finish**.

22. To create an IP security rule, click **Add**, click **Next** three times to accept the defaults, click the **All ICMP Traffic** option button, click **Next**, click the **Require Security** option button, click **Next**, click the **Use a certificate from this certification authority (CA)** option button, click **Browse**, click the **Issued to** column heading button twice to sort the entries, expand the column to view the names, scroll and click **Classroom Enterprise CA**, click **OK**, click **Next**, click **Finish**, and then click **OK** twice.

9

23. To activate the certificate policy, click **IP Security Policies on Local Computer** in the console tree, right-click **Certificate Policy** in the right pane, and then click **Assign**. Verify that the status in the Policy Assigned column changes to **Yes**.

24. To restart the IPSec Policy Agent, expand **Computer Management** in the console tree, expand **Services and Applications** in the console tree, click **Services** in the console tree, scroll and click **IPSEC Services** in the right pane, and then click the **Restart the service** hyperlink. If you receive the IP Security Monitor error message, click **OK**.

25. To reconnect the IP Security Monitor, expand **IP Security Monitor** in the console tree, right-click **STUDENT4** in the console tree, and then click **Reconnect**.

26. To verify that IPSec is being negotiated, return to the Command Prompt window, type **ping 192.168.1.2 –w 100** at the command prompt, and then press **Enter**. Your output should resemble the following listing:

```
C:\Documents and Settings\Administrator.DOMAIN1>ping
192.168.1.2 —w 100

Pinging 192.168.1.2 with 32 bytes of data:

Negotiating IP Security.
Negotiating IP Security.
Negotiating IP Security.
Negotiating IP Security.

Ping statistics for 192.168.1.2:
    Packets: Sent = 4, Received = 0, Lost = 4 (100% loss),
```

27. To verify that IPSec is being used, type **ping 192.168.1.2 –w 100** at the command prompt, and then press **Enter**. Your output should resemble the following listing:

```
C:\Documents and Settings\Administrator.DOMAIN1>ping
192.168.1.2 —w 100

Pinging 192.168.1.2 with 32 bytes of data:

Negotiating IP Security.
Negotiating IP Security.
Reply from 192.168.1.2: bytes=32 time<1ms TTL=128
Reply from 192.168.1.2: bytes=32 time<1ms TTL=128

Ping statistics for 192.168.1.2:
    Packets: Sent = 4, Received = 2, Lost = 2 (50% loss),
Approximate round trip times in milli-seconds:
    Minimum = 0ms, Maximum = 0ms, Average = 0ms
```

28. To view the main mode details, return to the console window, expand **IP Security Monitor** in the console tree, expand **Main Mode** in the console tree, click **Generic Filters**, review the generic filter details in the right pane, click **Specific Filters** in the console pane, review the filter pairs in the right pane, click **IKE Policies** in the console tree, double-click **(Default)** in the right pane, review the policies for encryption and integrity, click **OK**, click **Statistics** in the console tree, review the counters in the right pane, click **Security Associations** in the console pane, review the security associations in the right pane, double-click **192.168.1.4** in the right pane, review the Me IP address and Peer IP address in the dialog box, review the selected security method(s), and then click **OK**.

29. To view the quick mode statistics, expand **Quick Mode** in the console tree, expand **Negotiation Policies** in the console tree, click **OK**, click **Statistics** in the console tree, and review the byte counts in the right pane. Close all open windows.

30. To reconfigure the IP address for STUDENT4, click **Start**, point to **Control Panel**, point to **Network Connections**, click **Local Area Connection**, click **Properties**, click **Internet Protocol (TCP/IP)**, click **Properties**, record the IP address, click the **Use the following IP address** option button, type the IP address recorded in step 3 of Lab 9.2 in the IP address field, press **Tab** to allow Windows Server 2003 to fill in the default subnet mask of **255.255.255.0**, type the DNS Server IP address recorded in step 3 of Lab 9.2 as the Preferred DNS server address, click **OK**, and then click **Close** twice.

31. To return the STUDENT4 server to a member of the Workgroup, click **Start**, right-click **My Computer**, click **Properties**, click the **Computer Name** tab, click **Change**, click the **Workgroup** option button, type **WORKGROUP** in the Workgroup text box, click **OK**, type **administrator** in the User name text box, type **secret** in the Password text box, and then click **OK**.

32. Close all open windows and shut down the STUDENT4 server.

33. Return to the STUDENT2 server. Close all open windows, clicking **No** in the Save the console dialog box, if necessary. Shut down the STUDENT2 server.

34. Return to the STUDENT1 server. Close all open windows, clicking **No** in the Save the console dialog box, if necessary. Shut down the STUDENT1 server.

35. To return the STUDENT4 server to the previous network, remove the data cable from the STUDENT4 server and attach the data cable used by the STUDENT4 server to the same hub used by the STUDENT3 server.

36. Log on to the STUDENT4 server as **administrator**. If the Logon to drop-down box is not displayed, click **Options**. Click the **Log on to** drop-down arrow, click **STUDENT4**, click in the Password text box and type **secret**, and then click **OK**.

37. To display the change the network identification, click **Start**, right-click **My Computer**, click **Properties**, click the **Computer Name** tab, and then click **Change**.

38. If Lab 9.2 Step 4 indicated that STUDENT4 is in a workgroup, click the **Workgroup** option button, click in the Workgroup text box and type **WORKGROUP**, click **OK**, type **administrator** in the User name text box, type **secret** in the Password text box, and then click **OK**. When the "Welcome to the workgroup" message appears, click **OK**. When the "You must restart this computer for the changes to take effect" message appears, click **OK**. Click **OK** to close the System Properties dialog box. When the "Do you want to restart your computer now?" message appears, click **Yes**, and then go to Step 40.

39. If Lab 9.2 Step 4 indicated that STUDENT4 was in a domain, click the **Domain** option button, type **domain1.classroom.com** in the Domain text box, type **administrator** in the User name text box, type **secret** in the Password text box, and then click **OK**. When the "Welcome to the domain1.classroom.com domain" message appears, click **OK**. When the "You must restart this computer for the changes to take effect" message is displayed, click **OK**. Click **OK**. When the "Do you want to restart your computer now?" message is displayed, click **Yes**.

40. Log on to the STUDENT4 server as **administrator** with the password **secret**.

41. Close all open windows and shut down the STUDENT4 server.

Certification Objectives

Objectives for Microsoft Exam #70-291: Implementing, Managing, and Maintaining a Microsoft Windows Server 2003 Network Infrastructure:

- Implement secure network administration procedures

- Monitor network protocol security

- Troubleshoot network protocol security

REVIEW QUESTIONS

1. You plan to use IPSec to secure communications between two computers running Windows Server 2003. When you define an IPSec policy rule, which three authentication methods can you use?

   a. Certificates

   b. Basic authentication

   c. Integrated Windows authentication

   d. Digest authentication

   e. Kerberos

   f. Pre-shared key

2. You manage a computer running Windows Server 2003. You want to protect the data that is transferred between this computer and client computers with an IPSec policy. When configuring security methods for the policy, which integrity algorithms can you choose? (Choose all that apply.)

   a. 6-bit DES

   b. SHA1

   c. MD5

   d. MS-CHAP

   e. 3DES

3. Match the displayed information with the location in the IP Security Monitor console tree.

___ 1. Active Policy	a. NAME OF THE POLICY
___ 2. Main Mode – Specific Filter	b. IP ADDRESSES OF BOTH COMPUTERS
___ 3. Main Mode – Security Associations	c. CONFIDENTIAL BYTES SENT/RECEIVED
___ 4. Quick Mode – Statistics	d. IPSEC RELATIONSHIPS BETWEEN BOTH COMPUTERS

REMOTE ACCESS

Labs included in this chapter:

♦ Lab 10.1 Installing and Configuring a RRAS Server

♦ Lab 10.2 Configuring a RRAS Client

♦ Lab 10.3 Configuring Remote Access Policies

♦ Lab 10.4 Configuring a Virtual Private Network (VPN)

Microsoft Exam #70-291 Objectives	
Objective	Lab
Configure Routing and Remote Access user authentication	10.1, 10.2, 10.3, 10.4
Implement secure access between private networks	10.1, 10.2, 10.3, 10.4
Troubleshoot user access to remote access services	10.1, 10.2, 10.3, 10.4

LAB 10.1 INSTALLING AND CONFIGURING A RRAS SERVER

Objective

The goal of this lab is to enable Routing and Remote Access Service (RRAS) to support remote access. In addition, a second goal of this lab is to configure RRAS options.

Materials Required

This lab will require the following:

- STUDENT1 and STUDENT2 server access

- A modem and a modem line for each server. (As an alternative, the connection can be provided with a null modem cable.)

Estimated completion time: **30 minutes**

Activity Background

Windows Server 2003 installs RRAS by default. However, you need to configure RRAS to enable it for use. The RRAS can be configured to be a router, a remote access server, or both. Because you will have an opportunity to complete labs on IP routing in a subsequent chapter, your current labs will focus on remote access.

Activity

ACTIVITY

1. With the power off on the STUDENT1 and STUDENT2 servers, connect the modems to the COM1 serial port on each server, and then power on the servers.

2. Log on to the STUDENT1 server as **administrator** with the password **secret**.

To remove a modem, click **Start**, point to **Control Panel**, click **Phone and Modem Options**, click the **Modems** tab, click the modem you want to remove, click **Remove**, click **Yes**, and then click **OK**.

NOTE

3. To open the Phone and Modems Options applet, click **Start**, point to **Control Panel**, and then click **Phone and Modem Options**.

4. If prompted, type *your area code* into the What area code (or city code) are you in now? text box, and then click **OK**.

5. To detect and install your modem, click the **Modems** tab, and then click **Add**. If necessary, clear the **Don't detect my modem; I will select it from a list** check box. Click **Next**.

6. Wait for your modem to be detected and installed. Click **Finish**, and then click **OK**.

7. To launch the RRAS console, click **Start**, point to **Administrative Tools**, and then click **Routing and Remote Access**.

 If RRAS is enabled (indicated by a green up arrow on the server), click **STUDENT1**, click **Action**, click **Disable Routing and Remote Access**, and then click **Yes**.

NOTE

8. To start the Routing and Remote Access Server Setup Wizard, click **STUDENT1** in the RRAS console tree, click the **Action** menu, click **Configure and Enable Routing and Remote Access**, and then click **Next**.

9. To enable a RRAS for remote and VPN dial-in, click the **Custom configuration** option button, click **Next**, click the **VPN access** check box to select it, click the **Dial-up access** check box to select it, click **Next**, review the summary, and then click **Finish**.

10. Wait for the configuration to complete. Click **Yes** to start the service. Wait for the RRAS to start. A green arrow should appear next to **STUDENT1** in the console tree.

11. To configure the IP address configuration, click **STUDENT1** in the console tree, click the **Action** menu, click **Properties**, click the **IP** tab, click the **Static address pool** option button, click **Add**, type **192.168.100.1** in the Start IP address text box, type **192.168.100.10** in the End IP address text box, click **OK**, click **Apply**, and then click **OK**.

12. To set the number of PPTP ports, right-click **Ports** in the console tree, click **Properties**, click **WAN Miniport (PPTP)**, click **Configure**, type **5** in the Maximum ports spin box, click **OK**, click **Yes**, click **Apply**, and then click **OK**.

13. To set the number of L2TP ports, right-click **Ports** in the console tree, click **Properties**, click **WAN Miniport (L2TP)**, click **Configure**, type **0** in the Maximum ports spin box, click **OK**, click **Yes**, click **Apply**, and then click **OK**.

10

14. To view the remote access and VPN ports, double-click **Ports** in the console. Review the right pane, which should resemble Figure 10-1.

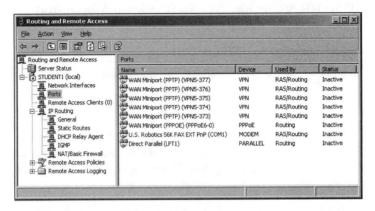

Figure 10-1 Remote Access and VPN ports

15. To review the authentication providers, right-click **STUDENT1 (local)** in the console tree, click **Properties**, click the **Security** tab, verify that **Windows Authentication** is displayed as the Authentication provider, and then click **Authentication Methods**. Your screen should resemble Figure 10-2.

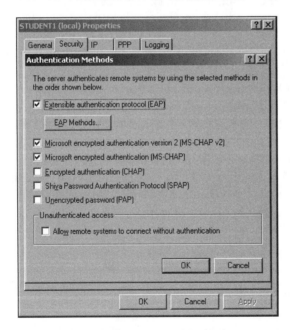

Figure 10-2 Authentication Methods

16. To review the EAP (Extensible Authentication Protocol) authentication methods, click **EAP Methods**, review the methods, click **OK**, and then review the remaining authentication methods. Verify that the **Microsoft encrypted authentication version 2 (MS-CHAP v2)** and the **Microsoft encrypted authentication (MS-CHAP)** check boxes are selected, click **OK**, click the **Accounting provider** drop-down menu, review the choices, verify that **Windows Accounting** is displayed as the Accounting provider, click **Apply**, and then click **OK**.

17. Remain logged onto the STUDENT1 server with the RRAS console open.

Certification Objectives

Objectives for Microsoft Exam #70-291: Implementing, Managing, and Maintaining a Microsoft Windows Server 2003 Network Infrastructure:

- Configure Routing and Remote Access user authentication

- Troubleshoot user access to remote access servers

REVIEW QUESTIONS

10

1. George has asked you about the features of a RRAS server. Which of the following will you point out to George? (Choose all that apply.)

   a. It permits mobile office workers to dial into a private network.

   b. It permits access to e-mail and Web servers.

   c. Universal naming convention (UNC) names are fully supported by remote access.

   d. The RRAS server authenticates the user.

   e. The network administrator cannot terminate a connection.

   f. VPN communicates across public networks such as the Internet.

   g. Remote access users cannot access network printers.

2. How do you enable routing and remote access on a Windows Server 2003 server?

   a. In the Network Connection Wizard, click Enable Routing and Remote Access.

   b. In the Routing and Remote Access console, click Configure and Enable Routing and Remote Access.

   c. Open the properties box for the WAN connection, and configure routing in the TCP/IP Properties dialog box.

   d. Open the properties box for the WAN connection, and then click the RRAS tab.

3. Sally configures her RRAS for remote connections. She views the RRAS console and discovers that she can view only VPN connections. She asks for your help. Which of the following will you suggest?

   a. Verify that the modem is attached.

   b. Reinstall RRAS to install the modem.

   c. Install a modem from the Phone and Modems Options applet.

   d. Configure the modem to accept incoming calls.

   e. Configure the RRAS to modem connector.

4. You configure the RRAS to use DHCP. The DHCP scope contains the 172.16.0.10 through 172.16.0.254 host address range. It is your understanding that the RRAS obtains 10 IP addresses from the DHCP server. The RRAS uses the first IP address obtained from DHCP for itself. The remaining addresses were allocated to TCP/IP-based remote access clients as they connected. You discover that the DHCP service was stopped on the DHCP server. Your remote access clients call to inform you that they cannot access resources on the 172.16.0.0 network. You check and see that the remote clients are connected with IP addresses in the range from 169.254.0.1 through 169.254.0.254. What item(s) do you suspect caused this problem? (Choose all that apply.)

   a. Subnet masks changed on the clients.

   b. APIPA addresses were used.

   c. Modems were restarted.

   d. RRAS service was restarted.

   e. The IP address of the DHCP server changed.

LAB 10.2 CONFIGURING A RRAS CLIENT

Objective

The first goal of this lab is to configure dial-in options for a user account requiring access to RRAS. After a remote access server is installed and configured, you will specify which users have remote access dial-in connection access. The second goal of this lab is to create and test a connection to RRAS with dial-up networking.

Materials Required

This lab will require access to the following:

- STUDENT1 and STUDENT2 server access

- A modem and a modem line. (As an alternative, the connection can be provided with a null modem cable.)

- Completion of Lab 10.1

Estimated completion time: **20 minutes**

Activity Background

To test dial-in access to the RRAS server, you must create a test user account. You will configure this account to permit dial-in access for given logon hours. From the Student2 server, you will test access to the Student1 RRAS server.

Activity

1. Verify that you are on the STUDENT1 server with the RRAS console open.

2. To open the Active Directory Users and Computers console, click **Start**, point to **Administrative Tools**, and then click **Active Directory Users and Computers**.

3. To open the new user dialog, expand **domain1.classroom.com** in the console tree, click **Users** in the console tree, click **Action** on the menu bar, point to **New**, and then click **User**.

4. Type **RAS** in the First name text box, press **Tab** twice, type **User** in the Last name text box, press the **Tab** key twice, type **RASUser** in the User logon name text box, and then click **Next**.

5. Type **Password1** in the Password text box, press the **Tab** key, type **Password1** in the Confirm password text box, clear the **User must change password at next logon** check box, click the **Password never expires** check box to select it, click **Next**, review the settings for RAS user, and then click **Finish**.

6. To allow remote access for the remote user, locate and right-click **RAS User** in the right pane, click **Properties**, click the **Dial-in** tab, click the **Allow access** option button, and then click **Apply**.

7. To set the logon hours for the RAS user, click the **Account** tab, click **Logon Hours**, click **All**, click the **Logon Denied** option button. Click the intersection of Monday and 6:00 am, drag across and down to the intersection of Friday and 8:00 pm, click the **Logon Permitted** option button, click **OK**, click **Apply**, and then click **OK**.

8. Minimize the Active Directory Users and Computers console. Remain logged on to the STUDENT1 computer with the RRAS console open.

10

9. Go to the STUDENT2 server. Log on as **administrator** with a password of **secret**.

10. To open the Phone and Modems Options applet, click **Start**, point to **Control Panel**, and then click **Phone and Modem Options**.

11. To detect and install your modem, click the **Modems** tab, click **Add**, if necessary, clear the **Don't detect my modem; I will select it from a list** check box, and then click **Next**.

12. Wait for the modem to be detected and installed. Click **Finish**, and then click **OK**.

13. To create a new dial-up connection, click **Start**, point to **Control Panel**, point to **Network Connections**, click **New Connection Wizard**, click **Next**, click the **Connect to the network at my workplace** option button, click **Next**, click the **Dial-up connection** option button, click **Next**, type **Course** in the Company Name text box, click **Next**, type *555-1234* in the Phone number text box, click **Next**, verify that the **Anyone's use** option button is selected, click **Next**, review the summary, and then click **Finish**.

14. To connect to the RRAS server, if necessary, clear the **Save this username and password for the following users** check box, type **RASUser** in the User name text box, type **Password1** in the Password text box, and then click **Dial**.

15. Wait for the connection to complete. Verify that the **Course is now connected** appears on the taskbar.

16. To review the connection status, right-click the **Dial-up Connection** icon in the taskbar tray, click **Status**, review the connection speed and time, and then view the sent and received bytes activity.

17. Click the **Details** tab, read the detailed information about the connection, including server type, transports, authentication, compression, and server and client IP address. Click **Close**.

18. To disconnect the communications, right-click the dial-up connection icon, and then click **Disconnect**.

19. Remain logged on to the STUDENT2 server. Return to the STUDENT1 server for the next lab.

Certification Objectives

Objectives for Microsoft Exam #70-291: Implementing, Managing, and Maintaining a Microsoft Windows Server 2003 Network Infrastructure:

- Configure Routing and Remote Access user authentication

- Troubleshoot user access to remote access servers

REVIEW QUESTIONS

1. Mike and Lillie discuss configuring user accounts for their future remote access users. They have asked you to clarify the options that can be set from the Active Directory Users and Computers snap-in for remote access users. Which of the following items are options within the snap-in that you will include in your discussion with Mike and Lillie? (Choose all that apply.)

   a. Permitted log on hours

   b. Remote access permissions for dial-out

   c. Remote access permissions for VPN

   d. Conditional remote access permissions for Dial-in

   e. Caller-ID to verify

   f. Callback options set by Caller

   g. Control access through Remote Access Policy

   h. User can change password

2. Susan is a contract programmer for your firm. She usually telecommutes from her home office. On occasion, she logs on to your RRAS and transfers completed program modules to the development groups server. Today she is working in a client's office. She connects to the RRAS. The RRAS accepts the call and then drops the call. You are called to resolve this problem. Which of the following will you consider to resolve this problem?

   a. The client's network does not support RRAS.

   b. The RRAS is set to call her home office.

   c. The client's office uses a different telecommunications carrier.

   d. The RRAS is set to use the caller-ID for her remote office.

   e. The modem in her laptop is defective.

   f. The remote charges for the call cannot be reversed.

3. Which of the following items can be viewed from the Details tab of the Dial-up Connection Status dialog box?

   a. Server type

   b. Transports

   c. Authentication

   d. Compression

   e. Client IP Address

10

Lab 10.3 Configuring Remote Access Policies

Objective

The goal of this lab is to configure remote access policy.

Materials Required

This lab will require access to the following:

- STUDENT1 and STUDENT2 server access

- Completion of Labs 10.1 and 10.2

Estimated completion time: **20 minutes**

Activity Background

As a network administrator, you can grant authorization using the dial-in properties of a user account or remote access policies. With remote access policies, a connection is authorized only if the settings of the connection attempt match at least one of the remote access policies. If the settings of the connection attempt do not match at least one of the remote access policies, the connection is denied regardless of how the dial-in properties of the user account are set.

Activity

1. Verify that you are on the STUDENT1 computer with the RRAS console open.

2. To start the Remote Access Policy Wizard, click **Remote Access Policies** in the console tree, click the **Action** menu, click **New Remote Access Policy**, and then click **Next**.

3. To allow domain users access to VPN, verify that the **Use the wizard to set up a typical policy for a common scenario** option button is selected, type **Allow VPN** in the Policy name text box, click **Next**, click the **VPN** option button, click **Next**, verify that the **Group** option button is selected, click **Add**, type **domain users** in the Enter the object names to select (examples) text box, click **Check Names**, click **OK**, and then click **Next**.

If you misspelled a domain name and an error message is displayed, click the **Remove** option button, and then click **OK**.

NOTE

4. To configure the authentication and encryption options, click the **Microsoft Encrypted Authentication version 2 (MS–CHAP v2)** check box to select it, click **Next**, clear the **Basic encryption (IPSec 56–bit DES or MPPE 40–bit)** check box, clear the **Strong encryption (IPSec 56–bit DES or MPPE 56–bit)** check box, verify that the **Strongest encryption (IPSec Triple DES or MPPE 128–bit)** check box is checked, click **Next**, review your settings, and then click **Finish**.

5. To start the Add Remote Access Policy Wizard, click **Remote Access Policies** in the console tree, click the **Action** menu, click **New Remote Access Policy**, and then click **Next**.

6. To allow domain users access, verify that the **Use the wizard to set up a typical policy for a common scenario** option button is selected, type **Allow Dial-In** in the Policy name text box, click **Next**, click the **Dial-up** option button, click **Next**, verify that the **Group** option button is selected, click **Add**, type **domain users** in the Enter the object names to select (examples) text box, click **Check Names**, click **OK**, then click **Next** three times, review your settings, and then click **Finish**.

7. To set the connection time parameters, right-click **Allow VPN** in the right pane, click **Properties**, click **Edit Profile**, click the **Minutes server can remain idle before it is disconnected (Idle–Timeout)** check box to select to it and change the value in the spin box to **30** minutes, click the **Minutes client can be connected (Session–Timeout)** check box to select it and change the value in the spin box to **30** minutes, and then click **Apply**.

8. To practice a multilink setting, click the **Multilink** tab, click the **Allow Multilink connections** option button, change the value in the Maximum number of ports allowed spin box to **3**, if necessary, change the value in the Percentage of capacity spin box to **50**, change the value of the Period of time spin box to **5 min**, click the **Require BAP for dynamic Multilink requests** check box to select it, and then click the **Do not allow Multilink connections** option button. (Recall that there is only one modem and that multilink requires more than one modem.) Click **Apply**, and then click **OK** twice.

9. To verify the domain functional level, restore the Active Directory Users and Computers window, click **domain1.classroom.com** in the console tree, click **Action** on the menu bar, and then click **Raise Domain Functional Level**. If you see the message "Current domain functional level: Windows Server 2003," click **Close**, and then go to Step 11.

10. To raise the domain functional level to support remote access policies, click **domain1.classroom.com**, click **Action** on the menu bar, click **Raise Domain Functional Level**, click the **Select an available domain functional level** drop-down arrow and click **Windows Server 2003**, click **Raise**, review the warning message, click **OK**, review the completion message, and then click **OK**.

10

11. To activate the remote access policy for the remote user, click **domain1. classroom.com** in the console tree, click **Users** in the console tree, locate and right-click **RAS User** in the right pane, click **Properties**, click the **Dial-in** tab, click the **Control access through Remote Access Policy** option button, click **Apply**, and then click **OK**.

12. Close the Active Directory Users and Computers console window.

13. Remain logged on to the STUDENT1 server with the RRAS window open.

Certification Objectives

Objectives for Microsoft Exam #70-291: Implementing, Managing, and Maintaining a Microsoft Windows Server 2003 Network Infrastructure:

- Configure Routing and Remote Access user authentication

- Troubleshoot user access to remote access servers

REVIEW QUESTIONS

1. Mike and Lillie discuss Windows Server 2003 RRAS authentication methods. They create the following list of valid authentication methods for Windows Server 2003 server. To help them out, arrange the methods in the order that a RRAS could use them, from most secure to least secure.

   1. MS–CHAP v2

   2. MS–CHAP

   3. CHAP

   4. PAP

   5. EAP

   6. Unauthenticated access

   a. 1, 2, 3, 4, 5, 6
   b. 5, 1, 2, 3, 4, 6
   c. 5, 2, 1, 3, 4, 6
   d. 1, 5, 2, 4, 5, 6

2. Samuel is concerned about carrier charges that are incurred by remote offices in the sales department. He wants to provide faster service by temporarily increasing bandwidth during the midmorning and midafternoon hours. At other times, he wants to throttle the bandwidth back. Which of the following would be the best solution for Samuel to implement?

   a. Change carriers.

   b. Use Multilink without BAP.

   c. Use Multilink with BAP.

   d. Use BAP without Multilink.

3. Which authentication protocol offers the most secure authentication for non-Microsoft clients?

   a. MS-CHAP v1

   b. MS-CHAP v2

   c. SPAP

   d. CHAP

   e. PAP

4. Which authentication protocol offers the most secure authentication for Microsoft clients?

   a. MS-CHAP v1

   b. MS-CHAP v2

   c. SPAP

   d. CHAP

   e. PAP

10

LAB 10.4 CONFIGURING A VIRTUAL PRIVATE NETWORK (VPN)

Objective

The goal of this lab is to create a VPN (Virtual Private Network) client that accesses a VPN server.

Materials Required

This lab will require access to the following:

- STUDENT1 and STUDENT2 server access

- A modem and a modem line. (As an alternative, the connection can be provided with a null modem cable.)

- Completion of Labs 10.1 through 10.3

Estimated completion time: **20 minutes**

Activity Background

You will use VPN to encrypt and transfer critical data across a simulated public network. The secondary goal of this lab is to review the dial-in connections to RRAS. As a network administrator, you manage and monitor connections to your RRAS server so that you can review which users are connected and obtain status information on a user. In this lab, you discover that the VPN connection is encapsulated within the dial-up connection. This is significant to you because this demonstrates that the second connection is "tunneling" over the first connection.

Activity

1. Verify that you are on the STUDENT2 server.

2. To create a new dial-up connection, click **Start**, point to **Control Panel**, point to **Network Connections**, click **New Connection Wizard**, click **Next**, click the **Connect to the network at my workplace** option button, click **Next**, click the **Virtual Private Network connection** option button, click **Next**, type **Course VPN** in the Company Name text box, click **Next**, verify that the **Automatically dial this initial connection** option button is selected and that Course is present in the drop-down list, click **Next**, type **192.168.100.1** in the Host name or IP address (for example microsoft.com or 157.54.0.1) text box, click **Next**, click the **Anyone's use** option button, click **Next**, review the settings, and then click **Finish**.

3. To dial in to the remote access server, click **Yes**, type **RASUser** in the User name text box, type the **Password1** in the Password text box, and then click **Dial** to complete the dial-up connection.

4. To log on to VPN, type **RASUser** in the Username text box, type the **Password1** in the Password text box, and then click **Connect** to complete the VPN connection.

5. To review the connection status for a dial-in connection, right-click the Course icon in the taskbar tray, click **Status**, read the connection time, and then read the bytes sent and received.

6. Click the **Details** tab, scroll and read the detailed information about the connection, and then click **Close**.

7. To review the connection status for a VPN connection, right-click the Course VPN icon in the taskbar tray, and then click **Status**.

8. To locate the IP address of the remote access server, click the **Details** tab, verify the detailed information about the connection, locate and record the server IP address, and then click **Close**.

9. Return to the STUDENT1 server.

10. To review the status of the remote access client connections, click **Remote Access Clients** in the left pane, and then review the connections in the right pane.

11. To review the dial-in connection status, right-click the first **DOMAIN1\RAS User** in the right pane, click **Status**, review the status, and then click **Close**.

12. To review the VPN connection status, right-click the second **DOMAIN1\RAS User** in the right pane, click **Status**, review the status, and then click **Close**.

13. To review the dial-in port status, click **Ports** in the left pane, right-click the modem connection, click **Status**, review the status, and then click **Close**.

14. To review the VPN port status, locate the active WAN miniport in the right pane under the Status field, right-click **WAN Miniport**, click **Status**, review the status, and then click **Close**.

15. To disconnect the VPN connection, right-click **WAN Miniport**, and then click **Disconnect**.

16. Click **Remote Access Clients** in the left pane, click the **Action** menu, click **Refresh**, and then verify that the remaining modem connection was disconnected in the right pane.

17. Close any open windows and shut down the STUDENT1 server.

18. Return to the STUDENT2 server, close any open windows and shut down the STUDENT2 server.

Certification Objectives

Objectives for Microsoft Exam #70-291: Implementing, Managing, and Maintaining a Microsoft Windows Server 2003 Network Infrastructure:

- Configure Routing and Remote Access user authentication

- Troubleshoot user access to remote access servers

Review Questions

1. Your boss has asked you to prepare a short presentation about VPN connections. Which of the following will be on the list of notes for your presentation? (Choose all that apply.)

   a. A dial connection is established.

   b. VPN requires an ISP to connect to the Internet.

   c. EAP supports the smart card.

   d. VPN packets are transported within PPTP.

   e. VPN requires MS–CHAP v2 authentication.

2. You install RRAS on a server. Your project calls for a remote user to connect with secure access to corporate files using the Internet. A database that will be made available to the public is present on the same server. Which RRAS protocol configuration would you chose?

   a. PPTP for the company's remote users and PPP for the general public

   b. TCP/IP for the company's remote users and PPTP for the general public

   c. PPP for the company's remote users and SLIP for the general public

   d. SLIP for the company's remote users and PPPMP for the general public

   e. PSTN for the company's remote users and X.25 PAD for the general public

3. Juan and Norma discuss VPN connections. Norma creates a list of possible steps for the VPN connection to a VPN server on the company's private network. They ask you to sequence the six steps in Norma's list. In what order would you put the following steps?

1. Client dials RRAS on a private network.

2. Client connects to virtual private network.

3. Remote access server authenticates the dial-up client.

4. Client and server conduct data transfers on an encrypted session.

5. Remote access server authenticates the client for the VPN connection.

6. Client disconnects the dial-up connection.

   a. 1, 5, 2, 3, 5, 6

   b. 1, 3, 2, 4, 5, 6

   c. 1, 2, 3, 4, 5, 6

   d. 1, 2, 3, 5, 4, 6

4. You have a bet with George. Which VPN tunneling protocol is supported on Windows Server 2003 using IPSec for data encryption through a logical tunnel? The correct answer determines the luncheon meal for the day. What will you be having for lunch?

   a. Hamburger: PPTP

   b. Pasta: L2TP

   c. Steak: MS-CHAP v2

   d. Salad: PPP

10

INTERNET AUTHENTICATION SERVICE

Labs included in this chapter:

♦ Lab 11.1 Installing and Configuring IAS

♦ Lab 11.2 Configuring RRAS as a RADIUS Client

♦ Lab 11.3 Configuring IAS as a RADIUS Proxy

Microsoft MCSE Exam #70-291 Objectives	
Objective	Lab
Configure Routing and Remote Access user authentication	11.1, 11.2, 11.3
Troubleshoot user access to remote access services	11.1, 11.2, 11.3

Lab 11.1 Installing and Configuring IAS

Objectives

The goal of this lab is to install and configure the Internet Authentication Service (IAS). You will also link IAS to Active Directory.

IAS is a Remote Authentication Dial-In User Service (RADIUS) Server. With IAS, you can centrally manage user authentication, authorization, and accounting. You can use it to authenticate users in Active Directory with your Windows Server 2003 domain controller. IAS supports a variety of network access servers, including RRAS (Routing and Remote Access Service).

Materials Required

This lab will require the following:

- STUDENT1 server access

- The Windows Server 2003 Installation CD-ROM

- Completion of Labs 4.1 through 4.5 and Labs 10.1 through 10.4

Estimated completion time: **20 minutes**

Activity Background

RADIUS is a client/server protocol that requires a RADIUS client and a RADIUS server to provide network access. STUDENT1, the domain controller with Active directory, will function as the RADIUS server. The RADIUS server will contact the Active Directory to make the determination of authentication and authorization. Microsoft recommends that the RADIUS server be installed on a domain controller to speed authentication.

In your configuration, STUDENT1 will serve as the RADIUS client. The RADIUS client will contact the RADIUS server when RRAS requests authentication and authorization. A Microsoft Windows 2003 server, which supports multiple services simultaneously, can be a RADIUS server, RADIUS client, and RRAS server.

Activity

1. Log on to the STUDENT1 server as **administrator** with a password of **secret**.

> **NOTE** To remove an existing installation of Internet Authentication Service, click **Start**, point **Control Panel**, click **Add or Remove Programs**, click the **Add/RemoveWindowsComponents** icon, locate and click **NetworkingServices** (the label and not the check box), click **Details**, clear the **InternetAuthenticationService** check box, click **OK**, click **Next**, click **OK**, click **Finish**, and then close the Add or Remove Programs window.

2. If needed, insert the **Microsoft Windows Server 2003 CD-ROM**; when the Microsoft Windows Server 2003 family window is displayed, click **Exit**.

3. To launch Add or Remove Programs, click **Start**, point to **Control Panel**, and then click **Add or Remove Programs**.

4. To install IAS, click the **Add/Remove Windows Components** icon, locate and click **Networking Services** (the label and not the check box), click **Details**, click the **Internet Authentication Service** check box to select it, click **OK**, click **Next**, wait for the files to copy and the configuration to complete, click **Finish**, and then close the Add or Remove Programs window.

5. To launch the Internet Authentication Service console, click **Start**, point to **Administrative Tools**, and then click **Internet Authentication Service**.

6. If needed, to enable IAS to read user objects in Active Directory, right-click **Internet Authentication Service (Local)** in the console tree, and then click **Register Server in Active Directory**. Wait for the "Register Internet Authentication Service in Active Directory" message, and then click **OK**.

7. To launch the Active Directory Users and Computers console, click **Start**, point to **Administrative Tools**, and then click **Active Directory Users and Computers**.

8. To verify permissions for the RRAS and IAS security group, click the **View** menu, click **Advanced Features**, expand **domain1.classroom.com** in the console tree, expand **System** in the console tree, right-click **RAS and IAS Servers Access Check** in the console tree, and then click **Properties**. Click the **Security** tab, click **RAS and IAS Servers (DOMAIN1\RAS and IAS Servers)**, and under **Permissions for RAS and IAS Servers**, verify that the **Allow** check boxes for **Read, Write, Create All Child Objects** and **Delete All Child Objects** are selected, and then click **OK**.

9. Close the Active Directory Users and Computers window.

> **NOTE** To remove an existing friendly name, click **RADIUS Clients** in the console tree, right-click **Course Remotes** in the right pane, click **Delete**, and then click **Yes**.

11

10. To register RADIUS clients, click **RADIUS Clients** in the console tree, click the **Action** menu, click **New RADUIS Client**, type **Course Remotes** in the Friendly name text box, type **192.168.1.1** in the Client address (IP or DNS) text box, click the **Next** button, verify **RADIUS Standard** in the Client-Vendor list box, click in the Shared secret text box and type **Windows Rules**, type **Windows Rules** in the Confirm shared secret text box, click the **Request must contain the Message Authenticator attribute** check box to select it, and then click **Finish**.

Passwords (shared secrets) are case-sensitive. Be sure that the client's shared secret and the shared secret are identical to each other and conform to the password rules.

TIP

11. To configure logging, click **Remote Access Logging** in the console tree, right-click **Local File** in the right pane, click **Properties**, click the **Settings** tab, verify that the **Accounting requests (for example, accounting start or stop)** check box is selected, verify the **Authentication requests (for example, access-accept or access-reject)** check box is selected, click the **Log File** tab, click the **IAS** option button, click the **When log file reaches this size** option button, record the name and location of the log file (your screen should resemble Figure 11-1), click **Apply**, and then click **OK**.

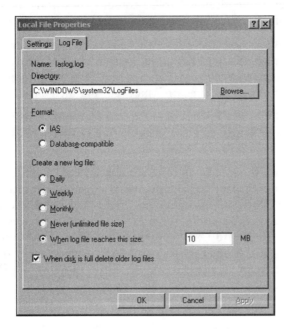

Figure 11-1 RADIUS logging enabled

12. To verify that the remote access policies are available, click **Remote Access Policies** in the console tree, and then verify that the **Allow Dial-In** is named first and **Allow VPN** is named second.

NOTE

Contact your instructor if the remote policies are not available.

13. Minimize the Internet Authentication Service console and remain logged on to the STUDENT1 server.

Certification Objectives

Objectives for Microsoft Exam #70-291: Implementing, Managing, and Maintaining a Microsoft Windows Server 2003 Network Infrastructure:

- Configure Routing and Remote Access user authentication

- Troubleshoot user access to remote access services

REVIEW QUESTIONS

11

1. You are preparing for the next study group meeting. Which of the following will you present to your peers regarding the characteristics of IAS?

   a. compatibility with RADIUS servers from other vendors

   b. integration with Active Directory for single user logon

   c. uses standards-based strong authentication

   d. accepts or rejects requests based on remote access policies

   e. supports RRAS as a NAS

2. You need to have a record of the user logons and logoffs for your RRAS servers. Which IAS settings will you select?

   a. logon requests

   b. logoff requests

   c. accounting requests

   d. authentication requests

   e. log requests

3. You are concerned about the authentication performance of your RADIUS server. To provide optimum performance, which of the following would be the best decision?

a. Install IAS on a standalone server.

b. Install IAS on the RRAS server.

c. Install IAS on the domain controller.

d. Purchase a RADIUS appliance.

LAB 11.2 CONFIGURING RRAS AS A RADIUS CLIENT

Objectives

The goal of this lab is to configure RRAS to use a RADIUS client. When you configure the properties of the server running Routing and Remote Access, you select RADIUS authentication and accounting.

Materials Required

This lab will require the following:

- STUDENT1 and STUDENT2 server access

- Completion of Lab 11.1

Estimated completion time: **20 minutes**

Activity Background

In your configuration, STUDENT2 will function as the RRAS client. The RRAS client, STUDENT2, will contact the RRAS server, STUDENT1. In addition, STUDENT1 serves as the RADIUS Client and RADIUS Server.

ACTIVITY

Activity

1. Verify that you are at the STUDENT1 server with the Internet Authentication Service console open and minimized.

2. To launch the Routing and Remote Access security dialog box, click **Start**, point to **Administrative Tools**, click **Routing and Remote Access**, and then expand **Routing and Remote Access** in the console tree, click **STUDENT1 (Local)** in the console tree, click the **Action** menu, click **Properties**, and then click the **Security** tab.

3. To use RADIUS authentication, click the **Authentication provider** drop-down arrow, click **RADIUS Authentication**, click **Configure**, click **Add**, type **192.168.1.1** in the Server name text box, click **Change**, type **Windows Rules** in the New secret text box, type **Windows Rules** in the Confirm new secret text box, click **OK**, click the **Always use message authenticator** check box, (your screen should resemble Figure 11-2), and then click **OK** twice.

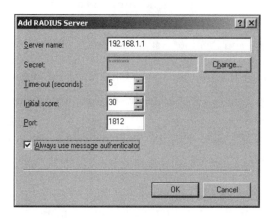

Figure 11-2   RADIUS authentication configured

4. To use RADIUS accounting, click the **Accounting provider** drop-down arrow, click **RADIUS Accounting**, click **Configure**, click **Add**, type **192.168.1.1** in the Server name text box, click **Change**, type **Windows Rules** in the New secret text box, type **Windows Rules** in the Confirm new secret text box, click **OK**, set the Initial score spin box to **30**, click the **Send RADIUS Accounting On and Accounting Off messages** check box, (your screen should resemble Figure 11-3), click **OK** twice, and then click **Apply**.

11

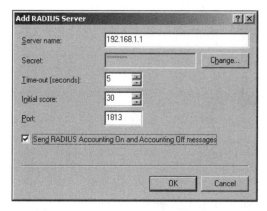

Figure 11-3   RADIUS accounting configured

5. If the "To use a new authentication provider, you must restart Routing and Remote Access" message appears, click **OK**.

6. If the "To use a new accounting provider, you must restart Routing and Remote Access" message appears, click **OK**, and then click **OK** again.

7. If a message appeared in Step 5 or Step 6, click **STUDENT1 (local)** in the console tree, click the **Action** menu, click **All Tasks**, and then click **Restart**. Wait for Routing and Remote Access to restart.

8. Go to the STUDENT2 server and log on as **administrator** with the password **secret**.

9. To connect to the Routing and Remote Access server, click **Start**, click **Connect To**, click **Course**, type **RASUser** in the User name text box, and then type **Password1** in the Password text box. Click the **Dial** button.

10. Wait for the connection to complete. Verify that the **Course is now connected** balloon appears on the taskbar.

11. To view the connection status, right-click the **Dial-up Connection** icon in the taskbar tray, click **Status**, view the connection speed and time and the sent and received bytes activity.

12. Click the **Details** tab, read the detailed information about the connection, including server type, transports, authentication, compression, and server and client IP address. Your screen should resemble Figure 11-4. Click **Close**.

Figure 11-4   Connection details

13. To disconnect the communications, right-click the **Dial-up connection** icon, and then click **Disconnect**.

14. Remain logged on to the STUDENT2 server.

Certification Objectives

Objectives for Microsoft Exam #70-291: Implementing, Managing, and Maintaining a Microsoft Windows Server 2003 Network Infrastructure:

- Configure Routing and Remote Access user authentication

- Troubleshoot user access to remote access services

REVIEW QUESTIONS

1. Which of the following forms of network access are supported by IAS?

   a. serial WAN connections (T-1)

   b. frame relay

   c. dial-up remote

   d. Virtual Private Networking (VPN)

   e. wireless

2. Ricardo is the network administrator for the Lonestar Flag Company. He is implementing RADIUS authentication for the three existing RRAS servers. He establishes the following goals for the project:

   - Support users in the lonestar.com domain

   - Permit users to use same accounts for remote and network logon

   - Use three existing RRAS servers

   Ricardo installs IAS on the AUSMS001 member server, which is a member of the lonestar.com domain. He verifies that the AUSMS001 server has been registered in Active Directory. Next, he creates a RADIUS client group called Allow Remotes that contains the names of the three RRAS servers. He enters and confirms the shared secret. For added security, he types a different shared secret at each of the three RRAS servers.

   Which of the goals will be achieved by Ricardo's implementation?

   a. Goal 1

   b. Goal 2

   c. Goal 3

   d. no goals are achieved

3. Which steps must you complete to successfully change from Windows Authentication to RADIUS Authentication?

   a. Open the properties dialog box for RRAS.

   b. Add the IP address of the RADIUS server.

   c. Add the IP address of the domain controller.

   d. Enter and confirm the secret.

   e. Check the RADIUS Accounting On and Accounting Off messages check box.

   f. Restart the RRAS service.

LAB 11.3 CONFIGURING IAS AS A RADIUS PROXY

Objectives

The goal of this lab is to configure a RADIUS proxy. IAS can be used as a RADIUS proxy to provide the routing of RADIUS messages between RADIUS clients (access servers) and RADIUS servers that perform user authentication, authorization, and accounting for the connection attempt. When used as a RADIUS proxy, IAS is a central switching or routing point through which RADIUS access and accounting messages flow.

Materials Required

This lab will require the following:

- STUDENT1 and STUDENT2 server access

- Completion of Labs 11.1 and 11.2

Estimated completion time: **15 minutes**

Activity Background

This lab adds the RADIUS proxy, which will contact the RADIUS server in behalf of RRAS. The server STUDENT1 is functioning in multiple roles (as a RRAS server, RADIUS Server, and a RADIUS proxy).

Activity

1. Verify that you are on the STUDENT1 server with the Routing and Remote Access console open.

2. Restore the Internet Authentication Service console.

3. To create a connection request policy, expand **Connection Request Processing** in the console tree, click **Connection Request Policies** in the console tree, click the **Action** menu, click **New Connection Request Policy**, click **Next**, type **Allow Course Remotes** in the Policy name text box, and then click **Next**.

NOTE To remove an existing connection request policy name, expand **ConnectionRequestProcessing** in the console tree, click **ConnectionRequestPolicies** in the console tree, right-click **AllowCourseRemotes** in the right pane, and then click **Delete**.

4. To specify the remote RADIUS server, verify that the **Authenticate connection requests on this server** option is selected, click **Next**, type **DOMAIN1** in the Realm name text box, clear the **Before authentication, remove the realm name from the user name** check box, click **Next**, and then click **Finish**.

5. Return to the STUDENT2 server.

6. To connect to the Routing and Remote Access server, click **Start**, click **Connect To**, click **Course**, type **RASUser** in the User name text box, and then type **Password1** in the Password text box. Click **Dial**.

7. Wait for the connection to complete. Verify that the **Course is now connected** balloon appears on the taskbar.

8. To disconnect the communications, right–click the **Dial-up connection** icon, and then click **Disconnect**.

9. Close all open windows, and then shut down the STUDENT2 server.

10. Return to the STUDENT1 server. Close all open windows, and then shut down the STUDENT1 server.

11

Certification Objectives

Objectives for Microsoft Exam #70-291: Implementing, Managing, and Maintaining a Microsoft Windows Server 2003 Network Infrastructure:

■ Configure Routing and Remote Access user authentication

■ Troubleshoot user access to remote access services

REVIEW QUESTIONS

1. Match the server type to the proper definition.

___ 1. IAS

___ 2. RADIUS server

___ 3. RADIUS client

___ 4. RADIUS proxy

    a. Performs authentication, authorization for its access clients

    b. Forwards incoming requests to specific servers for additional processing

    c. Performs authentication, authorization on behalf of a RADIUS client

    d. As a component of Windows Server 2003, performs centralized authentication, authorization, auditing, and accounting functions

2. Your company is currently using RADIUS. To gain a better understanding of how RADIUS functions, you observe the behavior of the various computers. You notice that a remote client (ComputerA) dials into a Windows Server 2003 (ComputerB). The Windows Server 2003 Server then passes the authentication information to another Windows Server 2003 (ComputerC) that is running IAS. In the above example, which of the following computers is the RADIUS client?

a. ComputerA

b. ComputerB

c. ComputerC

d. None of the computers in the above example are RADIUS clients.

3. Professor Boswell has lectured on RADIUS. You decide that your network could benefit from a RADIUS proxy. Which of the following will you include in the memo to your boss?

a. Use cross-forest authentication.

b. Provide load balancing.

c. Use connection policies.

d. Provide fault tolerance.

CHAPTER

12

ROUTING

Labs included in this chapter:

♦ Lab 12.1 Configuring Static Routes

♦ Lab 12.2 Configuring Dynamic Routing

♦ Lab 12.3 Implementing Demand-Dial Routing Connections

Microsoft MCSE Exam #70-291 Objectives	
Objective	Lab
Manage TCP/IP routing	12.1, 12.2, 12.3
Troubleshoot Routing and Remote Access Routing	12.1, 12.2, 12.3

LAB 12.1 CONFIGURING STATIC ROUTES

Objective

The goal of this lab is to configure static routes between two LAN segments. Routing is the process of forwarding packets between connected networks. Routing and other network protocol services provide forwarding capabilities between hosts that are located on separate network segments.

To implement IP routing, you need to understand the configuration of the routing table. Every server that runs the TCP/IP protocol makes routing decisions that are determined by the IP routing table.

Materials Required

This lab will require the following:

- STUDENT1, STUDENT2, STUDENT3, and STUDENT4 server access

- One additional hub and two data cables to connect the STUDENT1 and STU-DENT3 servers

Estimated completion time: **60 minutes**

Activity Background

In this lab, static routes control packet flow between the segments.

You will need to set up three LAN segments for IP routing. The first segment is allocated the address 192.168.1.0, the second segment is allocated 192.168.2.0, and the third segment, allocated 192.168.3.0, routes between the two existing networks.

Activity

1. To create the second physical segment for the routed network, install a hub, and then cable the secondary NICs in STUDENT1 and STUDENT3 to this hub.

Table 12-1 Server configuration parameters

Server	Adapter	Local Area Connection	Network Number	Adapter IP Address	Gateway IP Address	DNS IP Address
STUDENT1	Primary	-	192.168.1.0	192.168.1.1	None	192.168.1.1
	Secondary	2	192.168.3.0	192.168.3.1	None	192.168.3.1
STUDENT2	Primary	-	192.168.1.0	192.168.1.2	192.168.1.1	192.168.1.1
STUDENT3	Primary	-	192.168.2.0	192.168.2.1	None	192.168.2.1
	Secondary	2	192.168.3.0	192.168.3.2	None	192.168.3.2
STUDENT4	Primary	-	192.168.2.0	192.168.2.2	192.168.2.1	192.168.2.1

2. For the first server in Table 12-1, log on as **administrator** with the password **secret**.

3. For each local area connection in Table 12-1, click **Start**, point to **Control Panel**, point to **Network Connections**, right-click **Local Area Connection**, and then click **Properties**.

4. For each adapter in Table 12-1, click **Internet Protocol [TCP/IP]** (the label and not the check box), click **Properties**, click the **Use the following IP address** option button, type the indicated adapter IP address from Table 12-1 in the IP address field, press the **Tab** key, allow Windows Server 2003 to fill in the default subnet mask of **255.255.255.0**, type the indicated gateway address in Table 12-1 in the Default gateway text box, type the indicated DNS IP address in Table 12-1 as the preferred DNS server address, click **OK** twice, and then click **Close**.

5. Repeat Steps 2 through 4 for each remaining server in Table 12-1.

6. Return to the STUDENT1 server.

12

7. To verify the routing table in the STUDENT1 server, click **Start**, click **Command Prompt**, type **route print**, and then press the **Enter** key. Your output should have connected routes to the 192.168.1.0 and 192.168.3.0 networks, as follows:

```
C:\Documents and Settings\Administrator.STUDENT1>route print

IPv4 Route Table
===========================================================================
Interface List
0x1 ......................... MS TCP Loopback interface
0x10002 ...00 53 45 00 00 00 ...... WAN (PPP/SLIP) Interface
0x10003 ...00 b0 d0 52 8d 1c ...... 3Com 3C920 Integrated Fast Ethernet
Controller (3C905C-TX Compatible)
0x130004 ...00 08 c7 da b7 34 ...... Compaq NC3121 Fast Ethernet NIC
===========================================================================
===========================================================================
Active Routes:
Network Destination        Netmask          Gateway       Interface  Metric
        127.0.0.0        255.0.0.0        127.0.0.1       127.0.0.1     1
      192.168.1.0    255.255.255.0      192.168.1.1     192.168.1.1    20
      192.168.1.1  255.255.255.255        127.0.0.1       127.0.0.1    20
    192.168.1.255  255.255.255.255      192.168.1.1     192.168.1.1    20
      192.168.3.0    255.255.255.0      192.168.3.1     192.168.3.1    30
      192.168.3.1  255.255.255.255        127.0.0.1       127.0.0.1    30
    192.168.3.255  255.255.255.255      192.168.3.1     192.168.3.1    30
    192.168.100.1  255.255.255.255        127.0.0.1       127.0.0.1    50
        224.0.0.0        240.0.0.0      192.168.1.1     192.168.1.1    20
        224.0.0.0        240.0.0.0      192.168.3.1     192.168.3.1    30
  255.255.255.255  255.255.255.255      192.168.1.1     192.168.1.1     1
  255.255.255.255  255.255.255.255      192.168.3.1     192.168.3.1     1
===========================================================================
Persistent Routes:
  None
```

8. To verify the routing table for STUDENT3, complete Steps 6 and 7 for the STUDENT3 server. Your output should include connected routes to the 192.168.2.0 and 192.168.3.0 networks.

9. For the first server in Table 12-1, return to the STUDENT1 server with the Command Prompt window open.

Table 12-2 Static routing

Server	Network	Gateway	Metric
STUDENT1	192.168.2.0	192.168.3.2	2
STUDENT2	192.168.2.0	192.168.1.1	3
STUDENT3	192.168.1.0	192.168.3.1	2
STUDENT4	192.168.1.0	192.168.2.1	3

10. To open a command prompt on the STUDENT2 or STUDENT4 server, click **Start**, and then click **Command Prompt**.

11. To set up a static route to the network, type **route add**, type the indicated Network IP address in Table 12-2, type **mask 255.255.255.0**, type the indicated Gateway IP address in Table 12-2, type **metric**, type the indicated metric in Table 12-2, and then press the **Enter** key.

12. Repeat Steps 9 through 11 for each remaining server in Table 12-2.

13. Return to the STUDENT4 server with the Command Prompt window open.

14. To test connectivity through the network to the remote host, type **ping 192.168.1.2** at the command prompt, and then press the **Enter** key. Your output should indicate consecutive successful pings to the STUDENT2 server.

15. For the first server in Table 12-1, return to the STUDENT1 server with the Command Prompt window open.

16. To delete the existing static route, type **route delete**, type the indicated Network IP address in Table 12-2, and then press the **Enter** key.

17. Repeat Steps 15 through 16 for each remaining server in Table 12-2.

18. Remain logged on to the servers with the Command Prompt windows open.

Certification Objectives

Objectives for Microsoft Exam #70-291: Implementing, Managing, and Maintaining a Microsoft Windows Server 2003 Network Infrastructure:

- Manage TCP/IP routing

- Troubleshoot Routing and Remote Access routing

12

REVIEW QUESTIONS

1. Peter has just completed a default installation of Windows Server 2003 on a computer with two network adapters. Which dynamic routing protocols are installed by default?

   a. none

   b. RIP

   c. OSPF

   d. RIP and OSPF

2. Review the following output of the route print command, and follow the instructions after the routing table.

```
C:\>route print
=====================================================
Interface List
0x1 ......................MS TCP Loopback interface
0x1000003 ...00 b0 d0 52 86 f0 . 3Com EtherLink PCI
=====================================================
=====================================================
Active Routes:
Network Destination        Netmask         Gateway
        Interface  Metric
        0.0.0.0              0.0.0.0      192.168.1.1
    192.168.1.2         1
        127.0.0.0          255.0.0.0      127.0.0.1
    127.0.0.1         1
      192.168.1.0    255.255.255.0      192.168.1.2
    192.168.1.2         1
      192.168.1.2  255.255.255.255        127.0.0.1
    127.0.0.1         1
    192.168.1.255  255.255.255.255      192.168.1.2
    192.168.1.2         1
        224.0.0.0          224.0.0.0      192.168.1.2
    192.168.1.2         1
  255.255.255.255  255.255.255.255      192.168.1.2
    192.168.1.2         1
Default Gateway:         192.168.1.1
=====================================================
Persistent Routes:
  None
```

Using the routing table as a guide, match the routing table entry with its description.

_____ 1. 127.0.01   a. network broadcast address

_____ 2. 192.168.1.1   b. local host loopback address

_____ 3. 192.168.1.2   c. default gateway

_____ 4. 192.168.1.0   d. interface

_____ 5. 255.255.255.255   e. network address

3. Lucy is the network administrator for a Windows 2003 network. She needs to add a new static IP route. Which of the following will she need to enter to add the new static IP route?

   a. network mask

   b. gateway

   c. vector

   d. interface

   e. metric

   f. distance

   g. destination

4. Robert is a network administrator for a small network with three subnets. He has configured two Windows 2000 servers to act as routers between the subnets. Because Robert is using the 192.168.0.0 class C private addresses, the subnet mask is 255.255.255.0.

   The subnets are connected as follows:

Router	NIC connected to	IP address for NIC
Router A	Network 20.0	192.168.20.1
	Network 21.0	192.168.21.1
Router B	Network 21.0	192.168.21.2
	Network 22.0	192.168.22.1

   Robert needs to add entry on Router A that connects the path from network 20.0 to network 22.0. What is the correct routing table entry that Robert must type?

   a. route add 192.168.22.0 mask 255.255.255.0 192.168.21.1 metric 2

   b. route add 192.168.22.0 mask 255.255.255.0 192.168.21.2 metric 2

   c. route add 192.168.22.1 mask 255.255.255.0 192.168.21.1 metric 2

   d. route add 192.168.22.1 mask 255.255.255.0 192.168.21.2 metric 2

12

LAB 12.2 CONFIGURING DYNAMIC ROUTING

Objective

The goal for this lab is to configure the Routing Information Protocol (RIP), which is designed for exchanging routing information within a small to medium-sized internetwork. RIP is a distance-vector routing protocol that uses the number of 'hop' counts to determine the best route.

Materials Required

This lab will require the following:

- STUDENT1, STUDENT2, STUDENT3, and STUDENT4 server access, as set up in Lab 12.1

- Completion of Lab 12.1

Estimated completion time: **20 minutes**

Activity Background

In this lab, RIP replaces the static routes used in Lab 12.1. RIP simplifies the maintenance of routing information required by the routers.

Activity

1. Return to the STUDENT1 server with the Command Prompt window open.

2. To launch RRAS with IP routing selected, click **Start**, point to **Administrative Tools**, click **Routing and Remote Access**, expand **STUDENT1 (local)** in the console tree, and then expand **IP Routing** in the console pane.

   To delete a previous configuration of RIP, right-click **RIP** in the console tree, click **Delete**, and then click **Yes**.

   NOTE

3. To add RIP as a routing protocol, click **General** in the RRAS console tree, click **Action** on the menu bar, click **New Routing Protocol**, click **RIP Version 2 for Internet Protocol** in the Routing protocols text box, and then click **OK**.

4. To add an interface for RIP, click **RIP** in the console tree, click **Action** on the menu bar, click **New Interface**, click **Local Area Connection 2**, and then click the **OK** button.

5. Return to the STUDENT3 server with the Command Prompt open.

6. To start the Routing and Remote Access Server Setup Wizard, click **STUDENT3 (local)** in the RRAS console tree, click **Action** on the menu bar, click **Configure and Enable Routing and Remote Access**, and then click **Next**.

7. To enable a RRAS for remote and VPN dial-in, click the **Custom configuration** option button, click the **Next** button, click the **VPN access** check box, click the **Dial-up access** check box, click the **Next** button, review the summary, and then click the **Finish** button.

8. To launch RRAS with IP routing selected, click **Start**, point to **Administrative Tools**, click **Routing and Remote Access**, expand **STUDENT3 (local)** in the console tree, and then expand **IP Routing** in the console pane.

9. To add RIP as a routing protocol, click **General**, click **Action** on the menu bar, click **New Routing Protocol**, click **RIP Version 2 for Internet Protocol** in the Routing protocols text box, and then click the **OK** button.

10. To add an interface for RIP, click **RIP** in the console tree, click **Action** on the menu bar, click **New Interface**, click **Local Area Connection 2**, and then click the **OK** button twice.

11. To view the RIP update counts, click **Action** on the menu bar, and then click **Refresh**. Review the counts in the details pane. You should see a count of the routing updates, specifically, the Reponses sent and Responses received. (This also is a good time to take a few minutes and think about lunch for tomorrow.)

12. Return to the STUDENT4 server with the Command Prompt window open.

13. To test connectivity to the remote host, type **ping 192.168.1.2** at the Command Prompt, and press the **Enter** key. Your output should indicate consecutive successful pings to the STUDENT2 server.

14. Remain logged on to the servers with the RRAS console and Command Prompt open.

Certification Objectives

Objectives for Microsoft Exam #70-291: Implementing, Managing, and Maintaining a Microsoft Windows Server 2003 Network Infrastructure:

12

- Manage TCP/IP routing

- Troubleshoot Routing and Remote Access routing

REVIEW QUESTIONS

1. You need to implement a network routing strategy for your network. What should you do?

   a. Implement IGMP on all router interfaces.

   b. Implement static routes on all router interfaces.

   c. Implement RIP version 1 on all router interfaces.

   d. Implement RIP version 2 on all router interfaces.

2. Professor Boswell has lectured on RIP routing. You prepare for the next study group meeting. Which of the following will you include in your presentation to the study group? (Choose all that apply.)

a. RIP is an exterior Gateway Routing protocol.

b. RIP routers pass routing tables every 30 seconds.

c. RIP is effective for small corporate networks.

d. RIP uses a hop count to determine the distance between networks.

e. RIP version 3 is the current implementation for RIP.

3. You are a networking administrator for a network consisting of 6 LAN/WAN segments. You have implemented static routes between the segments. The WAN segment between Dallas and Houston is connected by a 56Kb connection. You implement a 256Kb frame relay that parallels the 56kb connection. You add RIP to the routers at Dallas and Houston. You do not see any noticeable improvement for the traffic between Dallas and Houston. What is the solution for the problem?

a. Implement RIP version 1 to improve performance.

b. Remove the static routes between Dallas and Houston.

c. Configure RIP to use multilink to split the traffic between the two connections.

d. Disable the 56Kb connection to force the static routes to use the 256 Kb connection.

4. You are the network administrator for a network of seven subnets. Three Windows Server 2003 servers are configured as network routers with RIP. Each computer serves as a router for three subnets. Router123 is connected to Subnet1, Subnet2, and Subnet3. Router345 is connected to Subnet3, Subnet4, and Subnet5. Router567 is connected to Subnet5, Subnet6, and Subnet7. Although you install RIP on all three routers, employees who use computers on Subnet1 are unable to communicate with computers on Subnet7. What is the first step you should take on each router to ensure that computers on Subnet1 can communicate with computers on Subnet7?

a. Delete all static routes.

b. Enable router authentication.

c. Define the interface or interfaces that should use RIP.

d. For each router interface, configure the IP address of other routers connected to a common segment as default gateways.

LAB 12.3 IMPLEMENTING DEMAND-DIAL CONNECTIONS

Objective

The goal for this lab is to implement demand-dial routing, also known as dial-on-demand routing. By using a demand-dial interface, routers initiate a connection to a remote site when the packet to be routed is received by the router. The connection becomes active only when data is sent to the remote site. When no data has been sent over the link for a specified amount of time, the link is disconnected.

Materials Required

This lab will require the following:

- The STUDENT1, STUDENT2, STUDENT3, and STUDENT4 servers, as set up in Lab 12.1

- Completion of Labs 12.1 and 12.2

- A modem and a modem line for the STUDENT1 and STUDENT3 servers (optionally, the connection can be provided with a null modem cable)

Estimated completion time: **25 minutes**

Activity Background

12

In this lab, a demand-dial connection will route between the 192.168.1.0 and 192.168.2.0 networks. One network will dial the other when a network failure is simulated.

Activity

1. Go to the STUDENT1 and STUDENT3 servers, close all open windows, and then shut down the STUDENT1 and STUDENT3 servers. With the power off on the STUDENT1 and STUDENT3 servers, connect the modems to the COM1 serial port on each server, and then power-on the servers.

2. Go to the STUDENT3 server and log on as **administrator** with the password **secret**.

3. Go to the STUDENT1 server and log on as **administrator** with the password **secret**.

4. To launch RRAS, click **Start**, point to **Administrative Tools**, and then click **Routing and Remote Access**.

5. To enable LAN and demand-dial routing, click **STUDENT1 (local)** in the console tree, click the **Action** menu, click **Properties**, verify that the **LAN and demand-dial routing** option button is selected, and then click the **OK** button.

6. To verify that inbound and outbound connections are enabled, expand **STUDENT1 (local)** in the console tree, click **Ports**, click **Action** on the menu bar, click **Properties**, click the modem selected in Lab 10.1, click **Configure**, verify that the **Demand-dial routing connections (inbound and outbound)** check box is checked, and then click **OK** twice.

7. To start the Demand-dial Interface Wizard, click **Network Interfaces** in the console tree, click the **Action** menu, click **New Demand-dial Interface**, and then click **Next**.

8. To specify the demand-dial interface, type **STUDENT3Router** in the Interface name text box, click **Next**, verify that the **Connect using a modem, ISDN adapter, or other physical device** option button is selected, click **Next**, click the modem installed in Lab 10.1, click **Next**, type **555-1234** (or the number supplied by your instructor) in the Phone number or address text box, click **Next**, verify that the **Route IP packets on this interface** check box is checked, check the **Add a user account so a remote router can dial in** check box, and then click **Next**.

9. To add a static route, click **Add**, type **192.168.2.0** in the Destination text box, type **255.255.255.0** in the Network Mask text box, click **OK**, and then click **Next**.

10. To create the demand-dial user accounts, type **Password1** in the Password text box, type **Password1** in the Confirm password text box, click **Next**, type **STUDENT1Router** in the User name text box, type **DOMAIN2** in the Domain text box, type **Password1** in the Password text box, type **Password1** in the Confirm password text box, click **Next**, and then click **Finish**.

11. To establish a pool of IP addresses, click **STUDENT1 (local)** in the console tree, click **Action** on the menu bar, click **Properties**, click the **IP** tab, verify that the **Enable IP routing** check box is checked, verify that the **Allow IP-based remote access and demand-dial connections** check box is checked, click the **Static address pool** option button, click **Add**, type **192.168.100.1** in the Start IP address text box, type **192.168.100.10** in the End IP address text box, click **OK**, click **Apply**, and then click **OK**.

12. Go to the STUDENT3 server.

13. To launch the Phone and Modems Options applet, click **Start**, point to **Control Panel**, and then click **Phone and Modem Options**.

14. If needed, type your area code into the What area code (or city code) are you in now? text box, and then click **OK**.

15. If necessary, to autodetect and install your modem, click the **Modems** tab, and then click **Add**. If necessary, clear the **Don't detect my modem; I will select it from a list** check box. Click **Next**.

16. Wait for your modem to be detected and installed. Click **Finish**, and then click **OK**.

17. To launch RRAS, click **Start**, point to **Administrative Tools**, and then click **Routing and Remote Access**.

> If RRAS was previously configured, click **STUDENT3 (local)** in the console tree, click **Action** on the menu bar, click **Disable Routing and Remote Access**, and then click **Yes**.

NOTE

18. To configure RRAS, click **STUDENT3 (local)** in the console tree, click **Action** on the menu bar, click **Configure and Enable Routing and Remote Access**, click **Next**, click the **Custom configuration** option button, click **Next**, click the **Demand-dial connections (used for branch office routing)** check box, click the **LAN routing** check box, click **Next**, and then click **Finish**. When requested to start the RRAS service, click **Yes**.

19. To enable LAN and demand-dial routing, click **STUDENT3 (local)** in the console tree, click **Action** on the menu bar, click **Properties**, verify that the **LAN and demand-dial routing** option button is selected, and then click **OK**.

20. To start the Demand-dial Interface Wizard, click **Network Interfaces** in the console tree, click **Action** on the menu bar, click **New Demand-dial Interface**, and then click **Next**.

21. To specify the demand-dial interface, type **STUDENT1Router** in the Interface name text box, click **Next**, verify that the **Connect using a modem, ISDN adapter, or other physical device** option button is selected, click **Next**, click the modem installed in Lab 10.1, click **Next**, type **555-2345** (or the number supplied by your instructor) in the Phone number or address text box, click **Next**, verify that the **Route IP packets on this interface** check box is checked, check the **Add a user account so a remote router can dial in** check box, and then click **Next**.

22. To add a static route, click **Add**, type **192.168.1.0** in the Destination text box, type **255.255.255.0** in the Network Mask text box, click **OK**, and then click **Next**.

23. To create the demand-dial user accounts, type **Password1** in the Password text box, type **Password1** in the Confirm password text box, click **Next**, type **STUDENT3Router** in the User name text box, type **DOMAIN1** in the Domain text box, type **Password1** in the Password text box, type **Password1** in the Confirm password text box, click **Next**, and then click **Finish**.

24. To establish a pool of IP addresses, click **STUDENT3 (local)** in the console tree, click the **Action** menu, click **Properties**, click the **IP** tab, verify that the **Enable IP routing** check box is checked, verify that the **Allow IP based remote access and demand-dial connections** check box is checked, click the **Static address pool** option button, click **Add**, type **192.168.110.1** in the Start IP address text box, type **192.168.110.10** in the End IP address text box, click **OK**, click **Apply**, and then click **OK**.

12

25. To test the demand-dial connection, click **Network Interfaces** in the console tree, click **STUDENT1Router** in the right pane, click **Action** on the menu bar, click **Connect**, and then wait for the interface connection to disappear. If you get an error message, contact your instructor for assistance.

26. To disconnect the demand-dial connection, click **STUDENT1Router** in the right pane, click the **Action** menu, and then click **Disconnect**.

27. Return to the STUDENT1 server with the RRAS console open.

28. To disable the existing 192.168.1.0 network and simulate a network failure, click **Start**, point to **Control Panel**, point to **Network Connections**, right-click **Local Connection 2**, and then click **Disable**.

29. Return to STUDENT4 server with the Command Prompt window open.

30. To dial the demand-dial connection, return to the Command Prompt window, type **ping 192.168.1.2**, and then press **Enter**. Wait for the modem to connect.

31. To test connectivity to the STUDENT2 server with the ping command, press the **up arrow**, and then press **Enter**. You should see a successful echo reply. If not, try several additional times. If you are still unsuccessful, contact your instructor.

32. Return to the STUDENT1 server.

33. To enable the existing 192.168.1.0 network, click **Start**, point to **Control Panel**, point to **Network Connections**, click **Local Connection 2**, and then wait while the network connection is enabled.

34. To disable the dial-up connection, return to the RRAS console, expand **IP Routing**, click **Static Routes** in the console tree, click **192.168.2.0** in the right pane, click **Action** on the menu bar, click **Properties**, clear the **Use this route to initiate demand-dial connections** check box, and then click **OK**.

35. Return to the STUDENT3 server with the RRAS console open.

36. If necessary, disconnect the demand-dial connection, click **Network Interfaces** in the console tree, click **STUDENT1Router** in the right pane, click **Action** on the menu bar, and then click **Disconnect**.

37. To disable the dial-up connection, click **Static Routes** in the console tree, click **192.168.1.0** in the right pane, click **Action** on the menu bar, click **Properties**, clear the **Use this route to initiate demand-dial connections** check box, and then click **OK**.

38. Close any open windows, log off, and shut down each server.

Certification Objectives

Objectives for Microsoft Exam #70-291: Implementing, Managing, and Maintaining a Microsoft Windows Server 2003 Network Infrastructure:

- Manage TCP/IP routing

- Troubleshoot Routing and Remote Access routing

REVIEW QUESTIONS

1. You prepare for the next techshare meeting for your workgroup. You want to introduce demand-dial routing. Which of the following will you present as reasons to use demand-dial routing?

    a. You are concerned about security, and you want to use a permanent connection.

    b. You cannot afford the communications cost of a permanent connection.

    c. You need a backup for a permanent connection.

    d. You can cut down on communication charges by using the link only when data is available to transfer.

    e. You will need a hardware router to implement demand-dial routing.

2. Which of the following can be used for a demand-dial interface?

    a. a modem

    b. a Token Ring adapter

    c. a direct parallel cable

    d. an Ethernet adapter

    e. a VPN WAN miniport

3. You want to configure the Dallas server to make a one-way demand-dial connection with the Houston server. Which of the following tasks would you complete on the Dallas server to configure demand-dial routing?

    a. Enable demand dial routing on the Houston server.

    b. Enable demand-dial routing on the Dallas server.

    c. Add a user account for Dallas on the Houston server.

    d. Add a user account for Houston on the Dallas server.

    e. Configure the demand-dial interface at Houston to use the Dallas account.

    f. Configure the demand-dial interface at Dallas to use the Houston account.

12

4. Frank needs to create a two-way, initiated demand-dial routing connection from the Austin office router to the Dallas office router. Which of the following must Frank do?

    a. Configure the Austin router to initiate demand-dial connections to the Dallas office router.

    b. Configure the Dallas office router to receive demand-dial connections from the Austin office router.

    c. Configure the Dallas router to initiate demand-dial connections to the Austin office router.

    d. Configure the Austin office router to receive demand-dial connections from the Dallas office router.

5. You are asked to configure the demand-dial interfaces and user accounts for the company's two offices in Chicago and Dallas. Match the interfaces below with the correct user account names for a two-way, initiated, demand-dial routing connection between the two cities.

    ____ 1. Chicago demand-dial interface   a. Chicago router

    ____ 2. Chicago credential   b. Dallas router

    ____ 3. Dallas demand-dial interface   c. Chicago user account

    ____ 4. Dallas credential   d. Dallas user account

CHAPTER 13

SECURITY TEMPLATES

Labs included in this chapter:

♦ Lab 13.1 Configuring Computer Security with Templates

♦ Lab 13.2 Analyzing Computer Security

Microsoft Exam #70-291 Objectives	
Objective	Lab
Implement secure network administration procedures	13.1, 13.2

LAB 13.1 CONFIGURING COMPUTER SECURITY WITH TEMPLATES

Objectives

The goal of this lab is to install the baseline server security template. In addition, networking services will be protected by the network infrastructure security template.

Materials Required

This lab will require the following:

- STUDENT2 server access

Estimated completion time: **15 minutes**

Activity Background

You use predefined security templates as a starting point for creating security policies that are customized to meet your organizational requirements. You can customize the templates with the Security Templates snap-in. Once you customize the predefined security templates, you can use them to configure security on an individual computer by importing the template into Local Security Policy.

ACTIVITY

Activity

1. Log on to the STUDENT2 server as **administrator** with the password **secret**.

2. To add security templates to an MMC console, click **Start**, click **Run**, type **mmc** in the Open text box, and then click **OK**. Click the **File** menu, click **Add/Remove Snap-in**, and then click **Add**. In the Available Standalone Snap-ins list box, scroll and click **Security Templates**, and then click **Add**.

3. To add Security Configuration and Analysis, click **Security Configuration and Analysis** in the Available Standalone Snap-ins list box, click **Add**, click **Close**, and then click **OK**.

4. To create a server baseline template, expand **Security Templates** in the console tree, expand **C:\WINDOWS\security\templates** in the console tree, right-click **hisecws**, click **Save As**, type **Server Baseline** in the File name text box, and then click **Save**.

CAUTION

Do not apply the hisecdc template to a server or domain controller.

5. To specify the security warning title, expand **Server Baseline** in the console tree, expand **Local Policies**, click **Security Options**, scroll and double-click **Interactive logon: Message title for users attempting to log on** in the right pane, verify that the **Define this policy setting in the template** check box is selected, type **Warning: Use of this system is Restricted!** in the text box, click **Apply**, and then click **OK**.

6. To specify the security warning text, double-click **Interactive logon: Message title for users attempting to log on**, verify that the **Define this policy setting in the template** check box is selected, type **This system is for the use of authorized users only. Individuals using this computer system without authority, or in excess of their authority, are subject to having all of their activities on this system monitored and recorded by system personnel.** in the text box, click **Apply**, and then click **OK**.

7. To specify a security database, click **Security Configuration and Analysis** in the console tree, read the instructions in the right pane, right-click **Security Configuration and Analysis** in the console tree, click **Open Database**, type **Server Baseline Database** in the File name text box, click **Open**, click the **Clear this database before importing** check box to select it, click **Server Baseline.inf**, and then click **Open**.

8. To configure security for the server, right-click **Security Configuration and Analysis**, click **Configure Computer Now**, and then click **OK**. Wait for the configuration to complete.

9. Remain logged on to the STUDENT2 server with the MMC open.

Certification Objectives

Objectives for Microsoft Exam #70-291: Implementing, Managing, and Maintaining a Microsoft Windows Server 2003 Network Infrastructure:

13

- Implement secure network administration procedures

REVIEW QUESTIONS

1. You are preparing for the next study group meeting. You want to provide your peers with information on security templates. Which of the following will you include in your presentation? (Choose all that apply.)

   a. Use Security Templates to apply consistent security settings.

   b. Microsoft does not provide any security templates.

   c. Security templates provide seven categories of security settings.

   d. Use Security Configuration and Analysis to configure security settings.

   e. Use the MMC to access Security Configuration and Analysis.

2. You want to manage the interactive logon settings for a local security policy of a computer running Windows Server 2003. Which node in the local security policy should you use to manage interactive log-on settings?

   a. Local Policies, then Security Options

   b. Security Options, then Local Policies

   c. Local Policies, then Account Policies

   d. Local Policies, then Interactive Logon Policies

3. You need to configure security-related settings on a computer on which you installed Windows Server 2003. Before you can configure the settings with Security Configuration and Analysis, which task must you perform?

   a. Create a security database.

   b. Run secedit.

   c. Create a security template.

   d. Verify that the computer is governed by a Group Policy Object (GPO).

4. You continue with your configuration of security-related settings. As a part of the creation of the security database, which of the following must you accomplish?

   a. Copy a template.

   b. Export a template.

   c. Import a template.

   d. Import a database.

LAB 13.2 ANALYZING COMPUTER SECURITY

Objectives

The goal of this lab is to analyze the existing computer security against the security database created in Lab 13.1.

Materials Required

This lab will require the following:

- STUDENT2 server access

- Completion of Lab 13.1

Estimated completion time: **15 minutes**

Activity Background

You use Security Configuration and Analysis to compare the current state of system security against an analysis database. During creation, the analysis database uses at least one security template. If you choose to import more than one security template, the database will merge the various templates and create one composite template. It resolves conflicts in order of import; the last template that is imported takes precedence.

Security Configuration and Analysis displays the analysis results by security area, using visual flags to indicate problems. It displays the current system and base configuration settings for each security attribute in the security areas.

Visual Flag	Flag meaning
Red X	Defined in analysis database and the server, but the security settings do not match
Green flag	Defined in analysis database and the server, but the security settings do match
Question mark	The entry was not defined in the analysis database.
Exclamation point	The entry was not defined in the analysis database but does not exist on the server.
No highlight	The item is not defined in the analysis database or on the system.

ACTIVITY

Activity

1. Verify that you are logged on to the STUDENT2 server with the MMC open.

2. Scroll to and then collapse **Security Templates** in the console tree.

3. To analyze system security, right-click **Security Configuration and Analysis**, click **Analyze Computer Now**, and then click **OK**.

13

4. To view the analysis, expand **Security Configuration and Analysis** in the console tree, expand **Local Policies** in the console tree, click **Security Options** in the console tree, and then scroll and locate the policies configured in Lab 13.1. Your screen should resemble Figure 13-1.

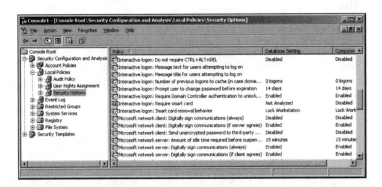

Figure 13-1   Security analysis results

5. To change the security database settings, expand **Account Policies** in the console tree, click **Password Policy** in the console tree, right-click **Minimum password length** in the right pane, click **Properties**, verify that the **Define this policy in the database** check box is selected, decrease the value in the Password must be at least spin box to **6** characters, click **Apply**, and then click **OK**.

6. To analyze system security, right-click **Security Configuration and Analysis** in the console tree, click **Analyze Computer Now**, and then click **OK**.

7. To view the analysis, expand **Account Policies** in the console tree, click **Password Policy** in the console tree, and then locate the icons with the red X. The red X should appear on the Minimum password length icon.

8. Close all windows and log off the STUDENT2 server.

Certification Objectives

Objectives for Microsoft Exam #70-291: Implementing, Managing, and Maintaining a Microsoft Windows Server 2003 Network Infrastructure:

- Implement secure network administration procedures

REVIEW QUESTIONS

1. You want to manage the assignment of security options in the security database of a computer running Windows Server 2003. Which node in the security database should you use to manage the user rights?

   a. Account Policies

   b. Local Policies

   c. Restricted Groups

   d. System Services

2. You want to set the password policy for your corporation using a GPO. How should you do this?

   a. Set password policy in the security template you create for your database, and in Security Configuration and Analysis in MMC, choose Configure Computer Now.

   b. Set password policy in the Security Settings, Local Policies area, of the User Configuration node at the domain level.

   c. Set password policy in the security template you create for your database, and in Security Configuration and Analysis in MMC, choose Analyze Computer Now.

   d. Set password policy in the Account Policy area of the Computer Configuration node at domain level.

13

3. You are analyzing the password policies of a Windows Server 2003 on your network. Figure 13-2 depicts the results of the analysis. What are your conclusions? (Choose all that apply.)

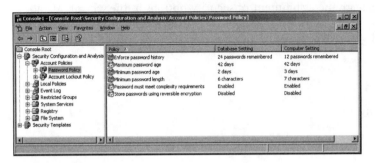

Figure 13-2   Analysis of password security

a. The computer setting for Password history is less than the password history for the database setting.

b. The computer setting for the maximum password age is 6 weeks.

c. The database setting for the minimum password length is 7 characters.

d. Users can change their password every 2 days.

e. Three potential problems were indicated.

14

TROUBLESHOOTING NETWORK CONNECTIVITY

Labs included in this chapter:

♦ Lab 14.1 Troubleshooting Server Services

♦ Lab 14.2 Monitoring Network Traffic

♦ Lab 14.3 Monitoring Network Performance

Microsoft MCSE Exam #70-291 Objectives	
Objective	Lab
Troubleshoot server services	14.1
Monitor network traffic	14.2, 14.3

Lab 14.1 Troubleshooting Server Services

Objectives

The goal of this lab is to troubleshoot Server Services.

Materials Required

This lab will require the following:

- STUDENT2 server access

Estimated completion time: **15 minutes**

Activity Background

As a network administrator, you need to troubleshoot dependent service failures. You will observe error messages that indicate that a service failed to start because a resource, such as a network card, was not available.

Activity

1. Log on to the STUDENT2 server as **Administrator** with the password **secret**.

2. To disable the network card, click **Start**, point to **Control Panel**, click **System**, click the **Hardware** tab, click **Device Manager**, scroll and expand **Network adapters**, right-click the first network adapter, click **Disable**, click **Yes**, verify that the icon has a red X, close Device Manager, and then click **OK**.

3. To restart the STUDENT2 server, click **Start**, click **Shut Down**, click the **What do you want the computer to do?** drop-down list arrow and click **Restart**, verify that the **Other (Planned)** option is selected, type **Disable Network Adapter** in the Comment text box, and then click **OK**. Wait for the server to restart.

4. Click the **OK** button when the "At least one service or driver failed during system startup. Use Event Viewer to examine the event log for details" message is displayed.

Since the network is not available, you must log on directly to the STUDENT2 server and not Domain1.

NOTE

5. Log on to the STUDENT2 server as **Administrator** with the password **secret**.

6. To launch Event Viewer, click **Start**, point to **Administrative Tools**, and then click **Event Viewer**.

7. To locate the dependent failure, click **System** in the console tree, scroll in the right pane and locate the error with the red X, and then double-click the error with the red X. If you do not see any errors, contact your instructor.

> To view additional error messages, click the drop-down list arrow in the Event
> Properties dialog box.

TIP

8. Click **Cancel** and close Event Viewer.

9. To enable the network card, click **Start**, point to **Control Panel,** click **System**, click the **Hardware** tab, click **Device Manager**, expand **Network adapters**, right-click the first network adapter, click **Enable**, wait for the network adapter to be enabled, close Device Manager, and then click **OK**.

10. To open Services, click **Start**, point to **Administrative Tools**, and then click **Services**.

11. To view DHCP client service dependencies, right-click the **DHCP Client** in the right pane, click **Properties**, and then click the **Dependencies** tab.

> The top list on the Dependencies tab identifies the other services that must be
> running for the selected service to function. The bottom list on the Dependencies
> tab identifies the services that require the selected service to be running so they
> can function.

NOTE

12. Click **OK**, and then close Services.

13. Remain logged on to the STUDENT2 server for the next lab.

Certification Objectives

Objectives for Microsoft Exam #70-291: Implementing, Managing, and Maintaining a Microsoft Windows Server 2003 Network Infrastructure:

- Troubleshoot server services

14

REVIEW QUESTIONS

1. Bob asks you to check on the status of the network card in the server on which he is installing Windows Server 2003. Which Windows Server 2003 tool will you use to determine if the network card is operational?

   a. Netcheck

   b. Device Manager

   c. IRQ Lister

   d. DEVMAN

   e. ipconfig

2. You install Windows Server 2003 on a computer. You use the typical network settings, which provide TCP/IP with a DHCP client. When you restart the computer, you receive the message "One or more services failed to start." You log in and use Event Viewer to look at the system log. You notice that none of your network services started. What is the most likely reason these services did not start?

   a. The network services are not configured to start automatically.

   b. The network adapter card settings conflict with the settings for another device.

   c. The computer could not contact a DHCP server.

   d. The network cable is unplugged.

3. You are troubleshooting the DNS client on a Windows Server 2003 computer. You need to determine which services must be started before the DNS client is started. What will be the correct sequence of steps to check for the DNS client service dependencies?

1. Click Start.

2. Click Services.

3. Point to Administrative Tools.

4. Click Properties.

5. Right-click DNS Client.

6. Click the Dependencies tab.

a. 1, 2, 3, 4, 5, 6

b. 1, 2, 3, 5, 4, 6

c. 1, 3, 2, 5, 4, 6

d. 1, 3, 2, 4, 5, 6

LAB 14.2 MONITORING NETWORK TRAFFIC

Objectives

The goal of this lab is to monitor network traffic with Network Monitor.

Materials Required

This lab will require the following:

- STUDENT1 and STUDENT2 server access

- Microsoft Windows Server 2003 CD-ROM

- Completion of Lab 14.1

Estimated completion time: **20 minutes**

Activity Background

As an administrator, you need to monitor and detect problems with traffic on your network. With Network Monitor, you can gather information about the network traffic that flows to and from the network adapter of the computer on which it is installed. Once you capture the information, you can use Network Monitor to analyze the information.

ACTIVITY

Activity

1. Verify that you are logged on to the STUDENT2 server.

2. Insert the Microsoft Windows Server 2003 CD-ROM in an available drive. When the Microsoft Windows Server 2003 family window is displayed, click the **Exit** hyperlink.

3. To open the command prompt for later network activity, click **Start**, click **Command Prompt**, and then minimize the Command Prompt window.

4. To install the network monitor, click **Start**, point to **Control Panel**, click **Add or Remove Programs**, click the **Add/Remove Windows Components** icon, scroll and click **Management and Monitoring Tools** (the label and not the check box), click **Details**, click the **Network Monitor Tools** check box, click **OK**, click **Next**, wait for the monitoring tools to be installed, click **Finish**, and then close the Add or Remove Programs.

5. To launch Network Monitor, click **Start**, point to **Administrative Tools**, and then click **Network Monitor**. Click **OK** to acknowledge the "Please specify the network on which you want to capture data" message, expand **Local Computer**, click **Local Area Connection**, and then click **OK**.

6. To start a capture, click the **Capture** menu, and then click **Start**.

7. To simulate network activity, restore the Command Prompt window, type **ping 192.168.1.1 −n 10** at the command prompt, press **Enter**, and then minimize the Command Prompt window.

8. When you are done capturing frames, click the **Capture** menu and then click **Stop and View**.

9. To filter for the ICMP packets, click the **Display** menu, click **Filter**, click **Protocol == Any** in the Capture Filter window, click **Edit Expression**, click **Disable All**, scroll and click **ICMP**, click **Enable**, and then click **OK** twice.

10. Locate a frame of interest, and then double-click it. Review the information that the ping command created.

11. Close Network Monitor and click **No**. Leave the Command Prompt window minimized, and remain logged on to STUDENT2 for the next lab.

Certification Objectives

Objectives for Microsoft Exam #70-291: Implementing, Managing, and Maintaining a Microsoft Windows Server 2003 Network Infrastructure:

- Monitor network traffic

REVIEW QUESTIONS

1. You are a network administrator and you need to see the application packets that are sent from an application server. Which tool will you use?

   a. Computer Management

   b. Device Manager

   c. System Monitor

   d. Network Monitor

2. Professor Boswell lectured on the Microsoft Network Monitor. You are preparing to meet with your study group and want to be ready to discuss Network Monitor. Which items will appear in your outline regarding Network Monitor? (Choose all that apply.)

   a. Analyze protocols.

   b. Capture and display packets.

   c. Analyze network traffic patterns.

   d. Analyze server performance.

3. You get a question from Bob at work. He is using the Microsoft Network Monitor to capture packets on the research network. He is concerned about the volume of packets that he will need to review. What will you suggest to make Bob's task easier?

   a. Place a hardware router between the server and the network to filter packets.

   b. Utilize RRAS to filter the packets.

   c. Place a filter appliance between the server and the network to filter packets.

   d. Use the display filter to limit the number of packets.

4. Bob continues with his study of packets. He wants to know why he sees only the packets from and to his server. He voices his opinion that he should be able to see the packets from the other servers. What do you tell Bob about the Microsoft products that capture packets? (Choose all that apply.)

   a. The full version is shipped with Microsoft Systems Management Server (SMS).

   b. A "lite" version is included with Windows Server 2003 and contains a subset of the features that are available in the full version.

   c. Your server must have a network card that supports promiscuous mode.

   d. When client and server applications are on the same computer, there is no network traffic.

14

LAB 14.3 MONITOR NETWORK PERFORMANCE

Objectives

The goal of this lab is to monitor network performance with System Monitor.

Materials Required

This lab will require the following:

- STUDENT1 and STUDENT2 server access

- Completion of Labs 14.1 and 14.2

Estimated completion time: **15 minutes**

Activity Background

Monitoring network performance is an important part of maintaining and administering your Windows Server 2003 installation.

Activity

1. Verify that you are logged on to the STUDENT2 server with the Command Prompt window minimized.

2. To launch System Monitor, click **Start**, point to **Administrative Tools**, and then click **Performance**.

3. To open the Add Counters dialog box, click **System Monitor** in the console tree, click **New Counter Set** (first button on the toolbar), and then click **Add Counter** (eighth button on the toolbar).

4. To add a performance counter, click the **Performance object** drop-down list arrow, scroll and click **Network Interface**, scroll and click **Bytes Received/sec** in the Select counters from list box, click **Network Interface Card** in the Select instances from list box (where Network Interface Card is the card installed on your server), click **Explain**, read the explanation for the counter, and then click **Add**.

5. Scroll and then click **Bytes Sent/sec**, click **Network Interface Card,** read the explanation for the counter, click **Add**, and then click **Close**.

6. To simulate network activity, restore the Command Prompt window, type **ping 192.168.1.1 −n 100** and then press **Enter**. Minimize the Command Prompt window.

7. Return to System Monitor and view the displayed chart.

 To scale the chart, right-click the **Scale** column heading, click **Properties**, change the Scale value to **.001**, and then click **OK**.

TIP

8. Close the open windows. Log off and shutdown the servers.

Certification Objectives

Objectives for Microsoft Exam #70–291: Implementing, Managing, and Maintaining a Microsoft Windows Server 2003 Network Infrastructure:

■ Monitor network traffic

REVIEW QUESTIONS

1. You are a network administrator. You need to study the network traffic for an application server. Which tool will you use?

   a. Computer Management

   b. Device Manager

   c. System Monitor

   d. Network Monitor

2. You install the DHCP server service on a computer running Windows Server 2003. You want to determine the number of DHCP requests submitted to the DHCP server. What two utilities might you use to enable the collection of this information?

   a. Network Monitor

   b. Local Security Policy

   c. System Monitor

   d. Group Policy Editor

   e. DHCP console

14

3. Sharon is considering monitoring a Windows Server 2003 server. She wants to include counters that will measure network performance. Which of the following counters should Sharon implement? (Choose all that apply.)

a. Memory\Pages/sec

b. Processor\% Processor Time

c. Memory\Available Bytes

d. Physical Disk\% Disk Time

e. Network\Bytes Sent/sec

f. Network\Bytes Received/sec